D1403470

THE PERSIAN SAYING IN THE FRONT-COVER IMAGE
IS FROM A POEM BY HÂFIZ:

We have not come to this door
looking for greatness and glory.

THE CIRCLE OF LOVE

THE CIRCLE OF LOVE

LLEWELLYN   VAUGHAN-LEE

THE GOLDEN SUFI CENTER

First published in the United States in 1999 by
The Golden Sufi Center
P.O. Box 428, Inverness, California 94937.

© 1999 by The Golden Sufi Center.

Cover illustration by Tennessee Dixon.
Printed and bound by Thomson-Shore, Inc.

Library of Congress Cataloging in Publication Data
The Circle of Love / Llewellyn Vaughan-Lee
          p.   cm.
Includes bibliographical reference and index.
ISBN 1-890350-02-8 (pbk.)
1. Spiritual Life   2. Prayers   3. Meditation   4. Love
I. Title
BL624.V383   1999   99-24565
297.4'4--dc21   CIP

CONTENTS

Step out of the circle of time
And into the circle of love.

Rûmî

What security is there for us here in the caravanserei
when every moment the camel bells cry,
"Pack up the loads!"?

The dark night, the fear of waves,
the terrifying whirlpool,
how can they know of our state,
those who go lightly along the shore?

Hâfiz

INTRODUCTION

The people of love are loved through their love.

Bâyezîd Bistâmî

The mystical path is a journey from duality back to unity, back to the pre-eternal oneness that is hidden within the heart. For the Sufi this journey is a love affair that begins on the level of the soul and is brought into consciousness through the grace of the Beloved. Sufis are those who love Him for His sake, and who have come to taste the sweet oneness of this love in the very substance of their being. This love draws us back to Him, back to what always is, to the eternal moment which does not belong to time.

Walking the path of love is a circular journey in which we discover what was always here but hidden under the veils of illusion, under the coverings of the ego and the mind. Stepping onto the path is stepping into the closed circle of love in which "the end is present at the beginning." In the West we are so addicted to the notion of progress that we project this idea onto our spiritual life, and can become very confused by the dawning realization that He whom we seek is always with us, that we are always close to Him but do not know it. The spiritual path is a process of revealing this nearness, the intimacy of love that is always with us.

Because He is one, His relationship to His creation, His relationship to us, must be a relationship of oneness. There is nothing other than He, and we are a part of His eternal oneness. The difficulties of realizing this oneness come from the fact that the ego and the mind know only duality: our very notion of our individual existence is defined by our being separate. All the concepts with which we define our life are based upon the ego and the mind's illusion of duality. Yet the spiritual path begins on the level of the soul where lover and Beloved are one. It takes us from the duality of our seeming existence into this dimension of eternal wholeness. This arena of love is the circle of oneness in which we die to our notions of duality: the ego is left a bloody carcass slain by love.

The work of the wayfarer is to try to remain within the circle of love, to resist the ego as it attempts to drag us away. The practices of the path, remembrance, devotion, surrender, bring us back to oneness while breaking the patterns of the mind and lessening the power of the ego. Slowly we become more and more aware of the circle of love, of His love for us which is the substance of our need for Him. Gradually we feel His closeness and realize it is always present. He allows us to forget Him and then draws us back, making us painfully discover His presence. In longing we cry to Him, in tears we come to Him, until we realize that our tears are our closeness, the depth of our longing is the degree of our nearness.

The circle of love found within the heart is also the ocean of all life, because nothing can exist without His love. Part of the mystery of creation is that His oneness is hidden, the knowledge of His love is veiled. The wayfarer is born into the ocean of life, which is a place of forgetfulness until we are awakened and drawn to discover the soul's secret. Through His grace we are given a glimpse of life's miracle: the love that permeates everything. In the oneness of this love everything is included and we find the truth of our own nature.

Why do we need to walk the long, painful path to realize what we really are, "the face we had before we were born," to recognize the miracle of life and love? Why do we need to forget in order to remember, to lose in order to find? These are questions which are left behind at the circle's edge. The circle of love has its own ways in which forgetfulness and remembrance belong together, in which seeking and finding are equal illusions.

This path cannot be understood with the logical mind, but there is a logic of the heart which we can come to know. There are ways of oneness which we can follow, footprints of guidance in which to place our two feet. The circle of love can be grasped with a mind attuned to the frequency of His need for us, to the soul's call to witness Him. Always, the real step is into the unknown and unknowable, but we can be led to the edge of His emptiness and know we need to jump. We can come to know that our prayer is always present, and that His love for us is stamped into the heart.

In the circle of love there are no obstacles because everything is given. How can there be an obstacle when there is no duality? In this circle duality disappears as "we two are fused, poured into one mold."[1] This is the mold of His making, in which we are recognized and remade. Love draws us here, and sometimes seems to abandon us to the fire of our remaking. Because oneness does not recognize the ego, this transformation can be painful and bitter, evoking so many confusions, so much agony. But if we stay within love's circle, if we do not allow our doubts, resentments, and other figments of the ego to interfere and draw us away, then oneness can open our eyes.

Each in our own way we come to experience love's contradictions, know her sweetness and terror, her bliss and devastation. But the circle of love is before the beginning and after the end. It is where love knows herself and we are a part of this knowing. "He loves them and they love Him" is the substance of our heart, the fragrance of our soul. Entering the circle we are drawn into this sacred bond which gives meaning to life's pilgrimage, which alone allows us to live what is Real.

THE PRAYER OF THE HEART

*God Most High hath brought forth creation and said,
"Entrust Me with your secrets. If you do not do this,
then look toward Me. If you do not do this, then listen
to Me. If you do not do this then wait at My door. If you
do none of this, at least tell Me your needs."*

Sahl[1]

THE FIRST PRAYER

Why do we pray? What is the real nature of prayer?
The mystic knows that the essence of prayer is the
hidden secret, "I am He whom I love, He whom I love
is me." In the deepest prayer of the heart there is only
oneness, for when the heart is open and looks towards
God, He reveals His unity. In this state of prayer there
are a merging and melting that transcend the mind and
its notions of duality: the heart overwhelms us with His
presence which obliterates any sense of our own self.

These moments of prayer are moments of union
in which the lover is lost. The lover has stepped from
the shore of his own being into the limitless ocean of
the Beloved. We make this offering out of devotion and
selflessness, out of the heart's need to share its secret.
Standing on the shore, we call His name; we cry out our
need to be with Him, our need to talk with Him, to share
with our Beloved our troubles and joys. But when He
comes close, our words fade away, left behind with our
mind that has dissolved in His presence.

1

When love reveals its real nature we come to know that there is neither lover nor Beloved. There is no one to pray and no one to pray to. We do not even know that we are lost; we return from these states of merging only knowing that we gave ourself and were taken. Our gift of ourself was accepted so completely that we knew nothing. We looked towards Him and He took us in His arms, embraced us in oneness, dissolved us in nearness. For so many years we cried to Him, we called to Him, and when He came the meeting was so intimate that we knew nothing.

But when we return from this merging of oneness, when the mind again surrounds us, we can see the footprints that led us to this shore, to the place where the two worlds meet. We can tell stories of the journey that led us to the edge of the heart's infinite ocean, of the nights we called to Him, and the tears we cried in our calling. For so many years our need was all that we knew, a need born of the despair of separation, the deepest despair known to the soul.

This need was our first prayer, planted in the soul by Him who loves us, who wants us for Himself. This need of the soul is the bond of love, the mystic's pledge to remember Him. The awakening of this remembrance is the knowledge of our forgetfulness, the knowledge of separation. The lover is made to know that she is separate from her Beloved, that she has forgotten Him. Awakening to this knowledge, the lover brings into consciousness the soul's need to return Home, to journey from separation to union. The first prayer is the sigh in the soul, the reed's lament that it has been torn from the reed bed and longs to return.

This first prayer is deep within us, and we feel it often blurred and indistinct, as the mind and ego block us from the potency of its message. Buried in the heart, in the innermost chamber of the heart, lover cries to Beloved, and we feel the echo of this cry as an unhappiness, a discontent. Subtly we are tormented by this call, and often try to avoid it, to run away from its primal sorrow. The world is full of so many distractions, the mind and psyche full of so many patterns of avoidance. But gradually, or in some cases suddenly, we know that we have to go Home, that we have to honor our longing, that we need to bring the prayer of the heart into our consciousness.

What began in the heart is passed to the tongue: "Oh Beloved, help me. I am so alone and I need you." The prayer is then made conscious, is incarnated with the word. With all the power and limitations of language, we speak our need, and so come to know our despair. We make conscious the pain of separation, and so call to Him even more, knowing in the depths that "I respond to the call of the caller when he calls to Me" (Qur'an 2:186).

This prayer, born of need, is so simple, giving voice to the heart's pain. Each in our own way we make this prayer; we bring into time and space the soul's sigh. And each time we pray, each time we call upon Him, we engrave this need more firmly into consciousness. The potency of the word is that it belongs to this world, to the world of separation. In the dimension of union there is no word; communication is communion, an unfolding of oneness. In the world of separation we need words, even to speak to our Beloved. When we speak to Him we acknowledge that we are separate and need Him. We state the gulf, the abyss between us. With each word we come to know our longing more consciously.

Sometimes we call with spontaneous prayer, *du'â'*, the free prayer of the heart, which is the intimate conversation of lovers. Or we may call with ritual

3

prayer, *salâh*, which for the Muslim mystic is a time of connection, "the moment of proximity to God."[2] In the words of Kharrâz, "When entering on prayer you should come into the Presence of God..., stand before Him with no mediator between."[3] Or we repeat the inward prayer of remembrance, the sacred syllables of the *dhikr*. In these ways we make known our need to call upon Him and to be with Him, make it known to ourself as well as to our Beloved. He knows we belong to Him, but with the words of our prayer we come to Him and remind ourself of His eternal presence. Our supplications remind us of our need to be nourished by Him alone.

Yet prayer, born of need, does not answer this need—it makes it more potent. We come to know more fully that we are separate, and that only He can help us. But to whom do we pray? To some idea of a distant God, a kind father figure, a nurturing mother? To someone who will wash away our tears and look after us, or even to an antagonistic tyrant? We personify our longing, clothe our tears in the image of a deity or lost love. In our weakness we look for strength, in our sorrow a comforting shoulder, in our pain a tormentor. Later, much later, we come to glimpse the closed circle of love, that our need is His need, that our cry to Him is His eternal answer: "Thy calling 'Allâh!' was My 'Here I am,' thy yearning pain My messenger to thee."[4]

We make an image of God to suit us, to give us comfort and security, to contain the pain of being human. But gradually all images fall away, for they too are veils of separation, denying the truth of union. How can He be separate from Himself? How can He call to Himself, long to return to Himself? The mystic is a part of this mystery, a mystery that can never be known to the mind and is even veiled from the heart.

In the closed circle of love He calls to Himself within the heart of His lover. Our need is His need, and yet He is complete in every way. We carry the seed of His longing and make it our own. Our very prayer to come closer to Him is an unfolding of intimacy, a sharing of something so precious that only His trusted servants are awakened to know it. To know that we need Him is to know that He needs us. He shares His longing with us. He calls to us and we call to Him, and so love reveals itself. What was hidden within the heart becomes part of everyday life, part of the texture of His world. We are burdened with the pain and bliss of sharing this secret, even though we can never fully know it.

PRAYER AND SURRENDER

Need is the beginning of prayer. Calling His name, crying out to Him, we make known our need to ourself and to Him. Need is the potency of our hidden love, and our prayer makes this love more visible, makes its fire burn stronger. Ibn 'Arabî prayed, "Oh Lord nourish me not with love but with the desire for love."[5] He knew that this desire would reveal what is hidden, would tear away the veils of separation. These veils isolate the lover, catching his attention in a world of multiplicity. Need turns us inward, away from these myriad reflections, towards the source, the oneness that is the root of our desire. But while we remain separate our need is also reflected in these veils, and so takes on different forms and qualities. All these forms we offer to Him in our prayers.

We pray according to our need, according to the need of the moment. Sahl said that "the prayer most likely to be answered is the prayer of the moment," "by which he meant the one the supplicant is forced to make because of the pressing need of what he prays for."[6]

At different moments our needs are different. We may pray for forgiveness, for understanding, for kindness. We may pray that our relationships not be clouded in mistrust or that our children not suffer. We pray for ourself and for others. All of the myriad difficulties that we encounter in our daily life we can embrace in our prayer, the difficulties of our own ego and the troubles of the world. We hope to bring His attention to these problems, so that His infinite grace can reach into His world and help with the pain of being human. He threw us into the world of separation where we need His help. The more we walk along the path, the more we realize how we are dependent upon Him, and the more we come to know the wonder of His mercy.

Prayer is infinitely powerful because it connects us with His infinite power. Praying to Him, we offer to Him the difficulties of living in a world of separation, in the deepest knowledge that only He can help us, He who is the source of all life and all love. We who are so small and alone look to Him, and so turn our attention from multiplicity back to oneness. Sometimes people think, "Why should I bother Him? How can my difficulties be of concern to Him?" But this is in fact arrogance, because it places the individual against God. In His oneness everything is included, everything is embraced. Nothing is other than He, and we are His eyes and ears in His world. In offering our sorrow, our difficulties, back to Him, we help Him to heal Himself, if it is His will.

Only if it is His will ... because prayer is an offering of surrender. Otherwise it is an act of will, a demand,

and a servant never demands. We look to Him, ask Him, implore Him, but do not demand. Always a prayer contains the heart's supplication, "If it is Thy will." Without this attitude of surrender the individual remains isolated, separate, and the prayer stays in the ego or the mind, where it is never heard. Through surrender we acknowledge a oneness greater than ourself, a oneness that brings help and mercy and grace unto itself. Healing and help come from within, from the source of all life that flows in the depths. What matters in all of our asking is that we call to Him and allow Him into our life. We turn from our separation to That which is not separate, to the One who is both the creation and the Creator, "both that which is drunk and he who gives to drink."[7]

"If the heart has heard the prayer, God has heard the prayer." The heart is the chamber of love's oneness, the infinite inner space where He is always present. Prayer leads us to the door of the heart. Surrendering to His will, we acknowledge His presence behind the door. We allow love to work according to its own ways. Rûmî tells a story of how He delays in answering the requests of those whom He really loves, while others He answers immediately:

> When two people, one decrepit and the other
>   young
> and handsome, come into a bakery where the
>   baker
> is an admirer of young men, and both of them
> ask for bread, the baker will immediately
> give what he has on hand to the old man.
>
> But to the other he will say, "Sit down and wait
>   a while.

There's fresh bread baking in the house.
    Almost ready!"

And when the hot bread is brought, the baker
    will say,
"Don't leave. The halvah is coming!"

So he finds ways of detaining the young
    man....[8]

Why does he make those whom He loves empty and destitute? Because He wants them to call upon Him. He loves to hear their voice. "It is related that Yahya b. Sa'id al-Qattan saw God in his sleep and exclaimed, 'O my God, how many times have I prayed to You and You have not answered me!' He said, 'O Yahya, this is because I love hearing your voice.'"[9]

If He answered our need fully and completely, we would no longer look to Him, no longer call to Him. He knows how to draw us to Him, "with the drawing of this Love and the voice of this Calling."[10] Through our prayers He calls us to Him, whether they appear to be answered or not. Surrendering to His will, we allow our prayers to carry the fragrance of His love back to us.

STANDING AT THE DOORWAY

Praying within the heart, we stand at the doorway between the two worlds, waiting for Him to help us. He who is our innermost essence is always there, eternally watching, listening, waiting for us to come to Him. We think He is separate, because we stand outside the door, caught in the world of duality. But when we pray with feeling, pray with the intensity of the heart, then the door opens. Actually this door is not closed; the ego only drew its veil across the threshold:

> Salih al-Murri said, "Whoever is persistent in knocking at the door is on the verge of having it opened for him."
>
> Râbi'a asked him, "How long are you going to say this? When was the door closed so that one had to ask to have it opened?"[11]

The intensity of our feeling takes us beyond the ego. Love hears our call and opens the door that is never closed. We are heard by our own heart, and our need is answered by love. Love is drawn by need, as Rûmî so poignantly writes:

> Not only the thirsty seek the water,
> the water as well seeks the thirsty.[12]

Love, the greatest power in the universe, does more than heal hearts. Love is the vehicle for His grace, the means of His mercy. Love brings both understanding and nearness, both wisdom and comfort.

Prayer is an ablution of the heart, for it takes us into the purifying stream of love that flows at the core of creation, the stream of "He loves them and they love Him" (Qur'an 5:59). In our prayer we are purified by our remembrance of Him rather than any desire for purity, as is beautifully imaged in the following dream:

> I am in the courtyard of a very ancient mosque. From an old black tap crystal clear water is running down on my hands, which are as if in prayer. I am having an ablution. The whole of me feels very ancient.... It is as if I am

inwardly merging into this beautiful water
while every atom in me is singing His prayer.
I become purer and purer.

In the sacred space of her own heart the dreamer
prays, and her prayer is an ablution, an ablution in
which the sacred water of her devotion runs down
onto her hands, purifying her. Hers is the deepest
prayer of merging, a prayer without words in which
she gives herself into her prayer so completely that
she hears every atom of her being singing His prayer.
The potency of her prayer is the purifying power of
love and devotion, a devotion that belongs to every
atom of herself. This is a prayer born of oneness that
carries the power of His love.

The heart evokes the deepest need of the soul, the
need to look to Him whom we love, to return from
duality to oneness. But in this world of separation the
heart's need can manifest in different ways, the prayer
of silence manifest into words. Lovers bring their needs
and the needs of others to the attention of their
Beloved. And when we pray with the intensity of real
need, either for others or for ourself, we attract His
love, we are carried into love. But when we pray for
ourself, it should not be for material matters, but for
the work of the heart, for understanding, compassion,
whatever may bring us nearer to our Beloved or help
us to serve Him. We do not pray for the ego and its
desires, because the prayer of the heart belongs to the
greater dimension of the Self. Prayer points us from
duality back to unity, but if we pray for the ego we are
caught in duality and separation.

Even when we pray for others, we need to be careful.
We can pray for healing, for guidance, for help in difficult
situations, an abusive relationship for example, but

should we pray for material things? It is not "wrong" to pray that someone find an apartment, or get a job, but only too easily is our attention caught in the material plane, which the mystic knows is a dance of appearances, a magic hall of mirrors that can teach us about ourself.

Often it is better to pray for understanding, for ourself and others, so that we can learn from a situation, rather than ask to change it. If we understand the teachings of an outer situation, apply our effort where it is needed, the situation will change of its own accord: a job will come to us. Life is the greatest teacher, and inner guidance can help us to catch the meaning of an outer situation, to learn the lesson it is trying to teach us so we don't have to repeat it. Walking the path between the two worlds, the way-farer knows the importance of taking inner responsibility for outer situations.

The sincere seeker is not interested in outer results, in success or failure, for she knows that life is a stage on which we have lessons to learn from our interaction with events and people. Prayer can help us to uncover the real meaning of an outer situation, and help us to stay with a situation, however difficult, until its deeper purpose is revealed. Otherwise, to quote T.S. Eliot, "we had the experience but missed the meaning."[13] Prayer, connecting us to our innermost self, can contain difficulties within the sphere of our own devotion, within the larger purpose of the soul. Offering to Him our problems, our unknowing, we know that we are heard somewhere. We know that a connection has been made to what is beyond time and space, beyond the conflicting opposites that cause us so much pain and confusion.

But this quality of prayer requires surrender and patience. We have to accept that we will know and understand only according to His will, not our own apparent need. We require patience to wait until the real meaning has unfolded, until we are allowed to know the deeper meaning of a situation and its means of resolution. And we have to trust what has been given and what will be given. This quality of surrender is an aspect of spiritual poverty, in which we acknowledge that we are in His hands and that only He can remedy our ills, only He can fulfill us.

BEING ATTENTIVE TO HIS NEEDS

Learning to ask with humility, patience, and poverty is also learning to listen. Within the heart we wait for His answer, for His words, even when we have not asked. Listening is a form of prayer, in which our whole being is receptive. Prayer is communion with God; we share with Him our needs, and we also learn to be attentive to His words, to His needs for us.

Listening within the heart is attuning ourself to our Beloved. We develop the ear of the heart, the inner listening of the soul. His words have a higher frequency than ordinary discourse; they are more subtle and easily overlooked. Listening requires both attentiveness and discrimination, as we have to discriminate between the voice of the ego and the voice of our Beloved. But there is a distinct difference: the words of the ego and mind belong to duality; the words of the heart carry the imprint of oneness. In the heart there is no argument, no you and me, just an unfolding oneness. The heart embraces a difficulty, while the ego takes sides.

Listening, waiting for His words, turns us away from our own needs to being attentive to His need. In our need we call to Him, and then we wait at the doorway of the heart, listening for His answer. But gradually, imperceptibly, this inner listening becomes more important than our own need. Our questions become fewer, our attention to Him grows. Once He begins to nourish us with His response, the soul's need for His company is nurtured, and the soul is no longer a starving infant crying in the darkness of abandonment.

We look to Him and He looks to us. Many times His response to our prayers is so deep or so subtle that we do not notice it—it is not captured by consciousness. But when we are made aware of His grace then the inner communion of the soul with its maker is brought into consciousness. Sometimes His response is a feeling, an increased awareness, an intuition. He may open our heart more fully, or touch the heart of another. His response may come to us in the outer world, a synchronicity that captures our attention, a change of situation, a healing that is given.

Sometimes He communicates directly with words. We may hear His words as a still, small voice, or a thought suddenly appearing. In meditation, when the mind is silent, we may hear His words of help and guidance. Or He may speak to us in dreams, when His words carry an energy that we know does not belong to our psyche, as when I was told that "He has a special tenderness for His own personal idiots." Sometimes we open a book we know and the words that we read are a message from our Beloved. In so many ways He speaks to us, answers our prayers, reveals Himself "on the horizons and in themselves."

When He speaks to us, hints to us, then we know we belong to Him, and we begin to feel the security of this belonging. His response carries the intimacy of this relationship. Even in the times of dryness, when He does not speak to us, we remember the imprint of His response. His actions carry the wonder of a miracle, His words the quality of divine consciousness. When He responds to us we know that He knows us, not just as part of the great mass of humanity, but as an individual, with our own unique needs. His infinite oneness comes to us in our aloneness.

We pray to Him and He answers. Knowing that our prayers are heard, we feel the wonder of knowing that the inner connection of the soul to God exists, not just as an abstract idea, but as a living reality. Being told that "God cares for us" is very different from experiencing the intimacy and individual nature of this care. His response brings into consciousness the soul's link to its Beloved. We experience the eternal as it becomes part of time and space, the vertical connection of the soul as it meets the horizontal plane of this world. We then no longer believe in God, we *know*.

When we know that He exists and cares for us, is attentive to us, we long to serve Him. That He should care for His servant awakens the servant's desire to serve Him. This desire to serve our master is imprinted into the soul, from the day of the primordial covenant, when God addressed the not-yet-created humanity with the words, "Am I not your Lord?" and humanity responded, "Yes, we witness it" (Qur'an 7:171). When this covenant is brought close to consciousness, it carries the wonder and numinosity that belong to the soul. Instinctively we bow before Him, and then know that we have bowed. We honor the soul's function to witness that He is Lord and we embrace our role as servant. The satisfaction that comes from living this primal relationship, from consciously enacting our role as servant, is deep and enduring. We bring our life onto the stage of the soul's relationship with its Creator.

Being attentive to His needs fulfills the real need of the servant. We are born to serve Him; this is our innermost nature. When the servant knows her role as servant and begins to live this attribute, a wonder, beauty, and depth of meaning permeate life. Listening to His needs and trying to meet them, we align our whole being with the soul's deepest purpose. Then the song of the soul can be heard in our daily life. The servant's need to serve her master is as deep as the need of the lover to reunite with the Beloved. Some Sufis would even say it is sweeter to serve Him:

> A thousand times
>   sweeter than Union
> I find this separation
>   You have desired.

> In Union
>   I am the servant of self,
> in separation
>   my Master's slave;
> and I would rather
>   be busy with the Friend
> whatever the situation
>   than with myself.[14]

Being attentive to the Beloved turns us away from ourself and back to Him. Our attention is held by the inaudible call of His presence and by our need to serve Him. Recognizing and then living our role as servant opens wide the door of the heart—the ego drops its defenses when we accept this deeper purpose. The servant looks to her master and He looks towards her:

"I have servants among my servants who love Me, and I love them, and they long for Me and I long for them and they look at Me and I look at them...."[15]

THE REFLECTION AND THE SOURCE ARE ONE

Our needs, our prayers, our supplications come from our despair at being separate. We need His mercy, His grace, His wisdom, His strength. We need to bring His qualities, His names and attributes, into our life. His response is to let us know these qualities within ourself, to find within our heart His wisdom, His forgiveness. The greatest illusion, the illusion of duality, that we are separate from Him, begins to dissolve as we taste and then live these qualities. Then we are embraced by the paradox that these divine qualities are other than ourselves and yet are a part of us. They belong to the Self and not to the ego. If the ego identifies with these qualities, then we suffer from inflation, feelings of grandeur and self-importance. But when the ego bows down before Him, when we become "less than the dust at His feet," then the servant can reflect the qualities of her Master. And within the heart the servant comes to know that the reflection and the source are one.

As the heart's prayer deepens, we pass from duality to oneness, and yet remain in the role of servant, knowing His divine otherness. To the mind this is a bewildering paradox, to the heart a simple truth. We have called to Him and He has answered; even in His silence He answered us. He *is* our call. Our confusion was that we did not recognize it. Surrendering in our prayers to His will, we recognize His omnipotence, and know that, because we are a part of Him, He fulfills His own need at the right time, in the right way. The simplicity of this revelation is overwhelming.

He needs us to call to Him so that He can come to know His own need. The more intense the call, the more full of feeling, the greater His need. We carry His consciousness in this world of duality—our consciousness is His consciousness (consciousness is His greatest gift to humanity). When we use this divine consciousness solely for the purposes of the ego, we remain within the ego, walled in separation. But when we use it for His purpose, so that He can hear the heart's need and other needs of His servants, then He reveals the oneness that is imprinted in this consciousness. He reveals the secret hidden within creation, hidden within our own hearts. Everything within the lover belongs to the Beloved, as Fakhruddîn 'Irâqî tells us:

> The lover's search and desire is but a sign of the Beloved's aspiration. Indeed, all his attributes—shame, desire, joy, taste, and laughter—everything he "owns" belongs in truth to the Beloved. The lover but holds it in trust; he cannot even be called a partner, for partnership in attributes would demand two separate essences. But in the lover's contemplative eye there exists in reality but a single Essence.
>
> > A hundred things
> > a million or more
> > if you look to their reality
> > are one.
>
> Thus all attributes pertain to the Beloved alone, leaving no ontological attribute to the lover. How could nonexistence possess the attributes of existence?[16]

The prayer of the heart lays this truth, the secret of secrets, at the feet of the Beloved. We have come to know His oneness, but in this experience there is no knower—we are not present. We give back to Him what He gave to us, the truth of His presence, the simple reality of His oneness. In this reality we are non-existent. The closed circle of love reveals its essential emptiness.

LISTENING

For all things
sing you: at times
we just hear them more clearly.

Rilke[1]

LISTENING IS A WAY OF BEING WITH GOD

Praying, we learn to listen, to listen to Him whom our heart loves. Yet listening is not an effort, not a technique; it is not work to be done. Listening springs from the desire to be with the one whom you wait to hear. Listening is a coming close, waiting for a presence to materialize into words, to form itself out of silence. Listening is a relationship, even in the silence when nothing is heard. Learning to listen is to allow ourself to be present without imposing or demanding, to hold a space where something can be told, where a meeting can unfold, where openness is answered.

There is a Chinese story of two friends, one who played the lute and the other who listened. The lute player was a wondrously skilled musician whose playing entranced all those who heard, and wherever he played, his friend sat and listened to his music. These friends were the closest companions, but one day the friend who listened died, whereupon the friend who played the lute so beautifully cut the strings of his lute and never played again. A lute with a cut string remains as a symbol of deep friendship.

The lover and Beloved are friends, and the lover is the one who listens, whose being is born to listen to his Beloved. Without the lover, how could the song of the Beloved be heard?

At the beginning we have to learn the art of listening, the art of being present, attentive, and empty. We have to learn to catch the still, small voice of our Beloved, and not interrupt, not ask too many questions. We have to learn to be silent, because listening is born from silence. But the listening of the heart is always an act of love, a coming together, even when nothing is heard. Listening is a wisdom so easily overlooked, because it is feminine, receptive, hidden, and our culture values only what is visible. But Rûmî knew how central a part it plays in our loving, in our wordless relationship with our Beloved:

> Make everything in you an ear, each atom of your being, and you will hear at every moment what the Source is whispering to you, just to you and for you, without any need for my words or anyone else's. You are—we all are— the beloved of the Beloved, and in every moment, in every event of your life, the Beloved is whispering to you exactly what you need to hear and know. Who can ever explain this miracle? It simply is. Listen and you will discover it every passing moment. Listen, and your whole life will become a conversation in thought and act between you and Him, directly, wordlessly, now and always.[2]

How can we learn this art of listening? How can we learn to hear what He says? How can we learn to be a part of His silence when nothing is said? How does the heart listen? What is listening within us? Is it always listening, but overlooked, obscured by all of our other activities? Or do we have to awaken this listening? Do we have to awaken each atom of our being to hear what the Source is whispering, or do we just have to attune ourself to this secret relationship?

Any real relationship is born out of similarity, affinity. Even if we appear to be opposite in many ways to our friend or partner, we are attracted by a similarity: this is our point of meeting. We share something, and the deeper the nature of what we share, the deeper and possibly more lasting the relationship. If we share just a passing interest, then probably the relationship will be passing. If we share an affinity of the soul, then the link is stronger, deeper, more enduring. With the Beloved we have the deepest similarity: we are made in His image. We are created out of His substance. In the depths of our heart we know that we belong to Him and have pledged to witness Him. This means that we have the deepest degree of communion with our Beloved, the deepest quality of listening. But like so much of our relationship with Him, our ability to listen to Him is covered up. Just as we have forgotten to remember Him, so have we forgotten how to listen, how to allow ourselves to listen. We need to rediscover how the heart listens to its Beloved.

THE RELATIONSHIP WITH THE TEACHER

One way that the wayfarer learns to listen is through the relationship with the teacher. This relationship is central to the Sufi path, because the teacher is the guardian of the gates of grace. Through her relationship with the teacher the wayfarer is taken into the presence of her Beloved; through the mystery of merging with the teacher she merges into the infinite emptiness of Allâh.

The teacher takes us into the infinite emptiness, and also teaches us how to attune to His presence when we are here, veiled in separation. Through the relationship with our sheikh we make a connection with Him whom our heart loves, Him in whose image we are made. Listening to the teacher, we learn to listen to what flows through the teacher, to the source from which he speaks. The teacher is one who has access to the source, who speaks as he is told. To quote Bhai Sahib, "I speak only as I am directed and only as much as I am told, not a word more."[3]

The work of the wayfarer is to listen and understand with a consciousness attuned to the teacher and the path. A Hermetic text describes this relationship between teacher and disciple:

> My child, it's your business to understand;
> it's my job to be successful at speaking the
> words that spring from the source which flows
> inside me.[4]

The work of the teacher is to speak, the work of the wayfarer to listen. Listening to the teacher, we listen not just to the words, but to the source from which he speaks. This requires a quality of attention both intense and subtle:

> My child, he who listens must perceive the
> same as he who speaks, share his awareness;
> he must breathe together with him, share the
> same spirit; his hearing must be sharper than
> the voice of him who speaks.

Now be completely present, give me your whole attention, with all the subtlety you can muster. For the teaching about divinity requires a divine concentration of consciousness if it's to be understood. It's just like a torrential river plunging headlong from the heights so violently that with its rapidity and speed it outstrips the attention not only of whoever is listening but also of whoever is speaking.[5]

Listening *is* attention; without attention there is no listening. Without this attitude of attention we may hear but not grasp the meaning of what we have heard, not realize its significance. Spiritual listening requires a conscious receptivity in which we hear not just the words but *from where the words come*. This attitude of receptivity is imprinted into the teacher; without it he could not teach. The teacher is consciously attuned to the source and receptive to its directions. Through giving her whole attention to the teacher the wayfarer can acquire this conscious receptivity—her attention enables this receptivity to be imprinted into her consciousness.

The teacher's attention is fixed on the invisible source, and the work of the wayfarer is to learn this quality of attention. Through giving her whole attention to the teacher the wayfarer learns to focus on what is within the teacher. Once the wayfarer's attention is fully fixed on the teacher, her attention can then be transferred to the essence of the path, the stream that comes from the source. Transferring the wayfarer back to the source is done by the teacher (something within the wayfarer is absorbed by something within the teacher). The work of the wayfarer is to remain focused on the teacher.

The wayfarer looks towards the teacher, listens to the teacher; the teacher listens to the source, is immersed in the source. The teacher is one who is merged, and finally this is what needs to be transferred to the wayfarer. The Hermetic text stresses the need for not only concentration but also a "sharing," or an affinity between teacher and disciple; he must "share his awareness ... share the same spirit." This is not detached listening, not the listening of an objective observer, but a listening that moves towards merging, a listening in which not only our ear but our whole being is with the one who speaks. How can we listen with the heart if we are detached? The heart only opens through intimacy, through closeness, through friendship and love. Listening with the heart, we come towards the one who speaks; we are drawn into the circle in which the source, the speaker, and the listener are united.

Within the heart is the consciousness of the Self, a quality of consciousness that belongs to oneness and not separation. When we listen with the heart we listen with this organ of oneness, in which at the deepest level we are already united with the source from which the teacher speaks. The communication of words, and what is behind the words, helps us to come to know what our heart already knows. This is why the listener has to give himself to the listening and to the one who speaks, and not stand separate, must "breathe together with him."

Listening with the heart, we hear the words and feel from where they come. We make a connection of oneness with the teacher. Listening to the teacher is a work of bringing the oneness of the heart into the consciousness of the mind, and thus coming to understand how oneness functions in a world of duality. In the words of the teacher we not only hear the underlying note of oneness, but also experience the dance of appearances. Listening to a Sufi, be prepared to be deceived! If you judge the outer appearance of what is said you may easily be misled, caught by what appears to be said. And thus you will miss the real meaning, the real message.

Sufis often speak in paradoxes, allusions, stories. What appears to be a silly story, a passing observation, may have deep meaning, or may just be a silly story. And what appears to be a profound teaching may indeed be profound, or may just be spoken to sidetrack the unprepared. Since meeting my teacher when I was nineteen, I spent many hours in Mrs. Tweedie's presence, listening to the web she wove, to the stories, pleasantries, and subtle insights that flowed. I watched visitors who were self-important being given a special chair beside her and encouraged to share their teaching with the group. I watched her allow dreams to be misinterpreted, or exaggerate incidents seemingly out of all proportion. Very often she would tell something to one person which was meant for another—speaking to the wall that the door might hear. And always for those listening there was the question, "What is really being said, and to whom?"

One time, when she felt that a seminar was full of people who had just come out of curiosity and were not really interested, she spent the morning saying how wonderful Margaret Thatcher and Ronald Reagan were, only too aware of the large number of left-wing socialists in the audience. During the lunch break many left in anger and disgust, so in the afternoon the atmosphere was right for her to talk esoteric Sufi philosophy. And when she was first invited to give a seminar in Switzerland, she spent two days telling jokes, bewildering the serious Swiss, who were not sure how to respond. But those who just laughed at the jokes did not grasp the poignancy of her teaching: how the path is always different from anything you might expect, because "whatever you think, God is the opposite of that." Underneath the laughter and confusion, she offered an experience of the path—not just words which are so easily forgotten.

People who expected "spiritual teaching" were given detailed stories of everyday events, long discourses on cats or the growing of roses. One friend came to meet Mrs. Tweedie after being in a spiritual group in which she felt that there was too much gossip. Mrs. Tweedie, unusually, was alone that day, and soon after this new visitor arrived she sat her down at the kitchen table. After serving her with a cup of tea, Mrs. Tweedie sat opposite her and said, "Now, let's have a really good gossip." Yet whole afternoons in the group were also filled with her speaking about her experiences with her teacher, and of a love that demands everything. She told us, "On the spiritual path one has to forget everything else," and quoted her sheikh: "One must not be distracted by non-essentials."

Listening with a mind attuned to the heart, the student learns to catch the meaning of what is said and what is not said, the subtleties of Sufi teaching. The words may mean just what they say, or the opposite of what they say, or something else altogether. What matters is that one listen not just to the words, but to the source from where the words come, to the interplay of the two worlds that is central to the Sufi path. The listener must participate, be open to deception as well as to what appears true. How do we know what is real by its appearance? Only when we have tasted the words can we feel from where they have come, on what level to understand them.

With a Sufi everything carries the same scent, the dance of the impossible and the hint of what is true. Only when you are a part of the dance can you catch its meaning, the subtle flow of its rhythm. Those who just observe can never feel what is conveyed. Sometimes we need to allow ourself to be deceived, led astray, because only then can we catch the deeper message, the source that speaks through the confusions. We have to catch the deeper significance of our life *as we live it,* amidst all of its deceptions. We have to catch what is hidden beneath the daily events of our life *as we enact them.*

Life is the greatest teacher, but also the greatest illusion. The Sufi teacher also plays these two parts, but with her very being points to what is real. My teacher spoke so often in contradictions and superficialities, as well as profound statements, but always there was a scent of something else. Those who looked only at the surface may have seen an old lady talking about the weather, the flowers in the garden, the symbolism of dreams, her love for her sheikh, while those immersed in the path sensed a hint of what can never be said.

Grasping the hint, the inner meaning of a situation, is a central teaching on the path, for "He has said, 'I have placed my signs on the horizons and in themselves.'" But we will never notice these signs if we see only what appears. The teacher *is* a sign: her very being is a pointer to something else, something that is lived and breathed in every cell of her body. And if we pay attention we can become attuned to this sign language, the way life hides its greatest mystery and reveals its real meaning. Listening to the teacher, we can learn to hear what is hidden. And once we grasp this inner meaning we have to hold onto it, to live it, be true to what we have found.

But at the same time not everything is a teaching, not everything has profound meaning. Sometimes a sincere student would look for unnecessary symbolism in Mrs. Tweedie's statements. If she asked with simple concern, "How are you?" the student would wonder what she really meant, what was the hint she was giving? Everyday life with all of its banalities is also a part of the Sufi way, and to always look for something deeper is also to be deceived. If life is lived from the source, the outer and the inner, the ordinary and the symbolic are combined. One evening a burglar tried to break into her apartment, and when she told the group about this the next day, one woman in the group, certain that such an incident must have a profound meaning, asked, "What does this mean?" She responded, "It means that a burglar tried to break in."

CATCHING THE DIVINE HINT

All of this work of listening, understanding, being deceived and confused is a process of preparation, like the tuning up of an instrument before a concert. The outer teacher always points to the inner teacher, to Him who is waiting within the heart of hearts. Through the relationship with our teacher we are prepared for this real relationship—through catching the hint in her words we are being trained to catch the divine hint:

> First one learns how to catch the hint of the Guru, and afterwards, when one is well merged, the Divine Hint, which is faster than lightning. The Guru will hint first; if the Hint is not understood, then he orders. An order is easy to understand, but the Guru trains the disciple to catch the Divine Hint rather. The Guru can give orders again and again if the disciple does not understand; but God does not do it, and the

Hint is lost, and one may wait for a long time
to get it again. To grasp it, one must be deeply
merged, so merged that one even looks for a
place to stand upon, for there seems to be
none....

To grasp a Hint is to act accordingly, and
not even to try to understand it. Acting accordingly is necessary, rather than understanding.[6]

Merging is one of the greatest mysteries of the
path: how the soul of the devotee is merged with the
soul of the sheikh (*fanâ fî'sh-sheikh*), and then merged
with the Prophet not as man but as Essence (*fanâ fî'r-
rasûl*), and then merged with Allâh (*fanâ fî Allâh*). Part
of the process of merging is a giving of oneself without
restrictions, surrendering beyond any boundaries.
Listening to the teacher, we give ourself, we surrender
any preconception, because only then can we grasp
the hint of what is said. Through this listening and
inner attention our heart is open to the heart of the
teacher and we can be taken into the stream of what
comes from the source.

Sufi teaching is almost always other than it appears,
because He is other than He appears. When we think
that we are listening to the words of the teaching, we
are opening ourself to what is deeper than words and
learning to be attentive to the source from which the
teacher speaks. If we really give ourself to listening we
cross over from being a separate observer into the
oneness of the real relationship with the teacher.
Listening takes us out of ourself, out of our seeming
separation, into the circle in which the words, the
speaker, and the listener are united. Leaving behind
any preconception, any attitude of "how it ought to

be," we enter into the space of real meeting, a meeting in which duality dissolves and we are merged.

Only from within this circle of merging are we able to catch His hint, "which is faster than lightning." The divine hint flashes into the heart, just at the boundaries of our consciousness, and is easily missed. Learning the art of listening to the teacher, we become attuned to the way the source speaks, so that when it speaks directly to us we are ready to catch it, and then live it without understanding, just "acting accordingly."

Living in the two worlds, bringing together the inner and outer, the mystic waits and listens, guided by His innermost voice:

> We obey orders. We lead guided lives. And this
> is the meaning to live in the ETERNAL NOW.
> We do not think of yesterday; we do not think of
> tomorrow; we listen within and act accordingly.[7]

In the eternal present of the path there is only the now, only the need of the moment. In this moment His need and our need are contained in the same circle. Living in the moment is a condition of vulnerability in which we are unprotected by past or future. We have stepped out of the duality of time, of past and future, and are able to listen and respond to the real need. In the eternal moment we belong only to Him.

We come to the path with so many preconceptions, so many ideas of "how it ought to be." Slowly our prejudices, especially our spiritual prejudices, are broken or dissolved; the ground under our feet begins to fall away. Only when we are suspended in space, with nowhere to stand, are we able to catch and respond to His hint, to its subtlety and speed, and enact it without hesitation, without the thoughts that come from preconceptions, or even a desire to understand. Listening to Him *is a state of surrender,* a surrender that is learnt through sacrifice and given through merging.

Something within us is awakened to listen to Him. We learn to be always attentive, always awake, always listening. Surrendering to Him, we experience being here for His sake, waiting for His will, ready to enact His will. We are here for Him because He needs us, and because we have pledged to witness Him. Waiting, listening, is an act of love, devotion, and commitment. We wait in poverty, the poverty of being without desires or preconceptions, the poverty of being empty of intention. We learn to be here for Him and in our everyday life. For Him there is no duality between the two, and we must honor His oneness. He is the source and the water that flows from the source. Through merging we come to know this oneness and something within us becomes attuned to Him and His needs.

TRUST

Learning to listen is not possible without trust. Without trust we are always on our guard; we have barriers of self-protection that defend us from what we cannot control. Listening is a state of openness; the more we are open the more we are able to hear. And because spiritual listening is done with the ear of the heart as well as our physical ears, the heart has to be open. Listening to the teacher requires a degree of vulnerability in which we lay down our defenses, we abandon our patterns of censorship. Listening to the Beloved means being totally open and surrendered; otherwise we will obscure His hint with our own self.

But how can we trust what we do not know? In everyday life we continually use trust in relation to our most basic activities. Turning the tap we trust that water will come out, booking an airline flight we trust that the plane will be at the airport and will take us to our destination. But this everyday trust is based upon tangible knowledge—we have seen the water flow from the tap. Also in these activities we are not exposing our deepest, most vulnerable self. Even when the airplane is not there at the airport (we have all heard of "mechanical failure"), we just have the inconvenience of waiting for the next plane.

In human relationships we learn the dangers of trust and the vulnerabilities of exposure. Here many of our wounds are born and our patterns of defense are created. We may come naked and defenseless into the world, but only too soon we feel the pain of our parents, the jealousies of our siblings, the attacks of our schoolmates. From the openness and instinctual trusting of an infant we learn the lessons of betrayal and wounding and develop our patterns of self-preservation, our walls of emotional defense. These patterns we then bring into the arena of our human loving, into any relationship that touches us beneath the surface.

But whatever the difficulties of trusting those whom we love, whom we want to love, at least there is someone there, another whose arms can embrace us, whose wounds we can learn to see. We can feel our way into the maze of our human loving, know when we are held and when we are rejected. We can also retreat inwardly, hide and defend ourself. Even in the most rapturous love affair, the most tragic relationship, we are separate from the one we love, and this separation is our greatest protection. When every outer trust is violated there is a place deeper than our wounding, a secret self in the very core of our being.

The spiritual path places two obstacles in the way of giving ourself to trust. First, there is no tangible object of our trust, and somewhere we are all a "doubting Thomas," the disciple who could not believe in the risen Christ until his hands had touched Christ's wounds. How can we trust what we can never see, or taste, or hear, or touch? How can we give ourself to what the mind can never know? Nor can we test this God in whom we are supposed to trust, and so often we test before we trust—we base our belief upon what we have come to know.

He demands that we give ourself to Him without proof or restrictions. And here a second obstacle stands in our way: the degree of the giving He demands. We cannot trust the Beloved "so far and no further." Trust in Him must be total or it is not trust. Trusting Him, we give ourself to a oneness that includes everything, even ourself. He is oneness, and He is not separate from us. When we give ourself to trusting Him there is no place to hide, no secret self to retire to. He is our secret self. He is the core of our being, just as He is every leaf of every tree. Because there is nothing other than He, to trust Him is a totality of giving that means absolute vulnerability.

For many people this degree of vulnerability is too threatening to even consider. Every cell of self-protection holds them back; every wound, every betrayal they have ever experienced says *No!* How can a human being expose herself to what she cannot touch, cannot know, and cannot limit? Every survival instinct screams against such unconditional, total trust.

But while our instinctual nature pulls us away from this brink, the soul knows the nature of His trust.

The soul longs to live this trust, to give itself to Him who can never betray us, who wounds us only to take us to Him, who embraces all of our life, from whom nothing is excluded. The soul's knowledge of His trust is given by Him; it is proof of His covenant with His creation. We bring it into this world as the will to worship Him and the need to give ourself in surrender to Him. And yet it is so difficult to live, to live His trust in us which in the circle of oneness we come to know as our trust in Him.

Here the relationship with the teacher helps, is a stepping stone to the relationship with our Beloved. The teacher is a tangible presence, and yet also lives a quality of the soul that belongs to the beyond. My teacher always said, "Do not trust me, the old lady you see sitting in front of you. Trust something else in me, the part of me that is somewhere else." The soul of the teacher is merged into her teacher, into the succession of superiors who belong to the path, who are the path. This is what the wayfarer needs to trust, never the physical presence of the teacher. For many wayfarers it is initially easier to trust a human being, someone upon whom we can project our own Higher Self, our own divine nature. This is all right at the beginning. But if we place too much trust in the outer form of the teacher we remain caught in appearances, and will usually end up feeling let down, rejected, or even betrayed. However, if the wayfarer grasps the real nature of the relationship with the teacher, trust in the teacher leads to trust in God.

The essence of the teacher is an empty space through which what is divine is able to manifest, to be heard, to be grasped by a heart attuned to love. The work of the teacher is to stay true to this inner emptiness, be attentive to the needs of the wayfarer and keep a connection with what is Real. Through this connection the wayfarer can learn to trust what cannot be seen, what cannot be touched, but can be felt within the heart, known within the soul. As the keeper of the gates of grace, the teacher helps the wayfarer come to know his or her own deepest trust in the Beloved.

Trust in God is a gift given by Him to help us come to Him, to help us step into the emptiness of His presence. Once we have tasted it, once we have come to know the nature of this trust, sensed its absolute quality—that it embraces everything—we cannot live without it. We can trust in Him so much more easily than in ourself or in our world. Only He is perfect, only He includes all aspects of ourself and our life. The path reveals our own inadequacies and failures, and it also shows us the illusory nature of the physical world. Why should we trust an illusion when we can trust what is Real? Why should we trust what is temporary when we can trust what is eternal? The spiritual path has its own logic, and although our mind cannot know Him, it can grasp the sense of trusting Him, of trusting in the Creator above the creation.

Personally I have always found it easier to trust God than to trust a person, to trust what is invisible and intangible than to trust this imperfect world. I can give myself to an invisible lover, to what is hidden within my heart, more securely than to any "other." While human relationships are caught in contradictions and the agony of duality, He is complete giving, and the heart knows this wholeness. Many others have this secret within their own heart, have been "branded by God" so that they can belong only to Him. At the right moment in their life the path awakens this knowledge, and slowly they come to know why in human loving they always feel inadequate.

He gives us the ability to trust Him, but we have to embrace the unknown in order to grasp it. We have to step from the ego to the Self. In order to be open we have to give ourself, write the blank check of our whole being. Some of us gave ourself long ago, but we still have to accept and then live this giving. We have to learn to listen to Him whom our heart knows, to allow our soul's openness into our daily life and come to know the vulnerability it demands. We have to allow our heart to be always open to hear His hint.

POWER & SPIRITUAL LIFE I
BREAKING FREE

*May God (whose name be exalted) grant success to
us and you in all that He desires and loves, of word
and deed, and theory and practice, and light and
guidance. Verily, He is over all things powerful and
fit to Answer.*

Ibn 'Arabî[1]

OWNING OUR OWN POWER

An impotent man or woman cannot realize the Truth.
The procreative instinct is a manifestation of the
creative energy of God, and this energy, which is the
most powerful thing in human beings, men and women
alike, is needed for the path.[2] Part of the initial work on
the path is to focus one's energy so that it can be used
for the process of realizing the Truth. On the Sufi path
sexual energy is not consciously transmuted, as for
example in Tantra, but its creative, instinctual source
is used. This instinctual energy can be experienced as
both power and passion.

Although Sufism is a devotional path of surrender,
this surrender is not passive, but a dynamic harnessing
of one's deepest energy source for the purpose of
transcending and transmuting the *nafs*, the ego and
lower nature. The primal power drive within a human

being is used for the sake of the Self, rather than for the purpose of ego desires. The wayfarer remains with desires like anyone else, only he is not the slave of these desires. Whether they are fulfilled or not is unimportant because a deeper purpose, the desire for Truth, has taken hold of him. While most people use their power drive to fulfill their ego desires, the wayfarer uses his power to realize the desire for Truth.

Growing up and adapting to our cultural conditioning is often a process of repressing power drives. We are taught to contain our desires within a socially acceptable framework, and this is necessary for the collective well-being of any community. Different communities foster the repression of different desires. For example, a culture of mountain warriors may encourage the fighting instinct but repress the sexual drive with strong cultural prohibitions, while a more "liberal" European culture may allow greater sexual freedom but have no place for the primal energy of the warrior. Also, in family dynamics certain energies are repressed for various reasons. For example, if one parent is overbearing and the other parent plays a victim role, then a child may repress her power drive rather than confront a family pattern, may even choose to also play the victim. The spiritual path involves releasing these repressed power drives and using them rather than being used by them. We become the master of our instinctual self and direct this energy towards the goal.

This energy needs to be first released and then used. Releasing one's instinctual power involves confronting the cultural taboo or family shadow dynamic that was the agent of repression. This is painful and demanding psychological work, as we descend into the darkness of the unconscious and face the figures or fears that have enchained us. The unconscious uses many and various methods to ensure our captivity, among them guilt, self-recrimination, and doubt. There is also the underlying fear of tasting our own power and then owning it. The pressures to remain to some degree a victim of our circumstances or ourself are in themselves very powerful. To step into the light of our own power demands courage and conviction, as a saying attributed to Nelson Mandela in his inaugural speech so potently expresses:

> Our deepest fear is not that we are inadequate. Our deepest fear is that we are powerful beyond measure. It is our light, not our darkness, that most frightens us. We ask ourselves, "Who am I to be brilliant, gorgeous, talented, fabulous?" Actually, who are you not to be? You are a child of God. Your playing small does not serve the world. There's nothing enlightened about shrinking so that other people won't feel insecure around you. We are all meant to shine as children do. We were born to make manifest the glory of God that is within us. It's not just in some of us; it's in everyone. And as we let our own light shine, we unconsciously give other people permission to do the same. As we're liberated from our own fear, our presence automatically liberates others.

Why is it so difficult to own our power? Because then we have to live it, to live from the depths of our own being and take responsibility for our actions. As long as we do not own our power, we can blame others, society, our parents, our partner, or even our children. But when we step into the circle of our own power, there is no one to blame, no one else to carry our convictions or our doubts. We are alone with our own destiny and the potential to live it.

Why should we want to avoid our own destiny, to live in the shadows of our own self? To fully embrace one's destiny is to stand alone before God in the arena of this world. Our fears contract us into the safe shadowlands with which we have become only too familiar. Life in the light threatens us with the unknown, the possibility of failure or, sometimes even more frightening, the fear of success. What happens if we live our deepest dream and don't make it? What happens if life does not answer our unacknowledged needs and there is no answer to our prayers? Or what happens if we transcend our limitations and step into the larger dimension of the Self? How will we open to the vulnerability and uncertainty of living in His light?

There are risks we must take, risks that are frightening but essential. There must come a call to step out of the darkness and then we must answer this call, answer it without caring for the consequences, for the obstacles of success or failure. Rûmî describes how this path is not for "brittle, easily-broken, glass-bottle people":

> A self-sacrificing way,
> but also a warrior's way, and not
> for brittle, easily-broken, glass-bottle people.
>
> The soul is tested here by sheer terror,
> as a sieve sifts and separates
> genuine from fake.
>
> And this road is full of footprints!

Companions have come before.
They are your ladder.
Use them![3]

Others have gone before us, have tasted the real
meaning of freedom and the bitter wind of Truth. They
leave behind their footprints and words of encourage-
ment, like Abu Sa'id who said so directly, "That which
is to be your fate, face it!" or the English mystical
painter Cecil Collins, "It is difficult to live a dream, but
even more difficult to live without a dream."

What is true and what is false? What are our real
convictions, our real destiny, our real need? Only when
we stand in the light of our own self can we separate
true from false, what belongs to us from what has been
forced on us or what we have been manipulated into
carrying. Then we can taste our own truth, what has
been imprinted into our soul. We can come to know
what we really are, and not what we have been told or
cunningly convinced we are. We are powerful beyond
measure because we are made in the image of Him
who is power beyond measure. We shrink from it
because we do not want to embrace our own divinity,
to carry the heart's conviction down whatever road
we choose to walk, wheresoever this destiny takes us.

Do we belong to others, to our parents, to our
friends or even to our enemies? Or do we belong to that
which has been hidden within us, sealed within the
heart? Do we have the courage to challenge the world,
to realize, "You guard the treasury of God's light—so
come, return to the root of the root of your own
self,"[4]—and then to live this hidden self, this inner light
in everyday life, despite all the misunderstandings that
will bombard us? Do we have the power to remember
what the world has forgotten, and live this remembrance

with each breath of our being? So much easier to remain in the half-light full of unlived possibilities, not even daring to acknowledge what we have lost.

CAUGHT BY CONDITIONING

One of the paradoxes of the inner journey is that the power we need to break through the patterns of conditioning is often locked within these very patterns. Our conditioning has spun its web so carefully that we are trapped, unable to find the energy we need to realize our own potential. The unconscious convinces us that we are helpless, and we accept the familiar pattern of our own impotence and dependency. Sometimes these patterns are woven so deeply that they seem to belong to centuries past, and carry the weight of a collective conditioning. The following dream carries an intense and painful feeling of victimization:

> I am imprisoned by a madman in a dark, grey, cavernous space. I am lying suspended here, up high, on a wooden platform. Floating in space is the maniacal face of the madman.
>
> Unspeakable tortures are inflicted upon me over and over again, which I don't recall. I just remember that it seemed like endless agony. Suddenly a woman is here, sent by the madman. She lies next to me, and at first acts sympathetic because she is also a woman. Then she is on top of me, and I know that she is truly allied to the madman.
>
> It is now, to my horror, that I realize that I am being raped. I think to myself, "Now I understand how rape is so horrible that a

person can only separate her consciousness completely from the experience, in order to remain true to herself in the midst of such horror." It is then that I blank out for a time.

When I regain consciousness I find myself way down, below ground level. I am completely alone and abandoned long, long ago, chained by my arms and legs to the bottom of a murky swimming pool. I feel as though I have been here for two hundred years.

The room is made of moldy white tiles with one high window which lets in stale light. The pool is dark and horrible. No one is in sight. It seems I am long forgotten, but I still fear that the madman's guards may be nearby.

But my desire to be free of him and free of this place and condition—*just to be free*—is so strong, so tremendous, that I thrust my fist up into the air, and to my amazement the chain crumbles off! It is so old. I thrust my other fist up and the same thing happens. I free my chained feet in the same way. I have freed myself with my desire to be free!

I don't care about the possible guards. *I have to be free.*

As I climb up onto the side of the pool I realize that I am completely naked, but I feel, "*I don't care.* If I have to walk naked down Main Street for the rest of my life, I don't care. I'm free and I'm never going back in there, ever again!"

Climbing out I see that the place has transformed into a lovely polished white marble space, lit from the ground up. A large arched doorway appears and I crawl outside.

For how long has this dreamer been a victim, suspended on a shelf in midair, chained in the waters of her unconscious? In this dream she experiences the terrible intensity and centuries-long suffering of her predicament, one that echoed within many of the women in our meditation group when she told this dream. She has been a victim, tortured by the masculine, whose maniacal head, floating in space, images the way masculine consciousness is so often cut off from the body. This disembodied quality of the masculine is in itself a painful torture for the feminine who carries the sacred wholeness of life in her body. But most painful is the rape by the feminine, by the woman in league with the dark power. This woman, acting sympathetic, comes to her full of pretense, full of the duplicity of her feminine self that has sold out to masculine values. The dreamer is raped by her own shadow, by her inability to value and live her true feminine nature. This situation echoes a dream another friend told, in which she is with another woman and two men come and want to use the dreamer as a prostitute. The dreamer doesn't want to be a prostitute but the other woman tells her that it is O.K., "she often does it, she just thinks of something else."[5]

Being raped by her own feminine self is more painful than anything the masculine can inflict, because it evokes a total helplessness and feeling of betrayal. So terrible is the dreamer's anguish that she has an intense desire just to escape her body and the woundedness of life. Trapped on a ledge with no way up or down, she is a total victim for whom the only escape is "to separate her consciousness from the experience." Then she blanks out, because the experience is too painful to accept—just as the other dreamer denies her experience of prostitution by "just thinking of something else." Each in our way we avoid consciously confronting and accepting our own impossible situations, the pain of our own incarnation—anything but realizing how fully we are trapped, how painfully violated. Yet in our avoidance we enchain ourself more fully, because consciousness is the only way to freedom. Unconsciousness is the greatest trap, even though it may appeal as a comforting escape.

In fairy tales the evil witch pricks the princess with her poisoned needle, and the girl falls asleep, drugged into unconsciousness. Here is the power of the negative feminine who weaves her web of unknowing, the comforting sleep of forgetfulness. Why suffer when you can forget? Why confront pain when it can be so easily avoided? In the desire to avoid what is almost unbearable, we sell the divine gift of consciousness for the safety of unconsciousness. This is the swimming pool of her own psyche in which the dreamer discovers she has been chained, chained for so long, for aeons. Patterns of avoidance can last for lifetimes, and also carry the pain of the collective. For how long has the feminine allowed herself to be chained by masculine values? How much suffering has she repressed over the centuries? In the intense anguish that can belong to a dream, the dreamer feels both her own pain and that of the collective, and finally, she decides to break free.

The decision to try with all her effort to break free is the turning point of the dream. She no longer accepts the dominance of the woman who raped her, the feminine who collaborates with the masculine. She no longer accepts her own impotence. The power of unconsciousness lies in making us believe that we can't do it, we can't change the patterns that imprison us. We are convinced by our conditioning, by the shadow, and so remain chained, up to our neck in the water of the unconscious.

The unconscious does not want her victim to become free; she does not want us to gain our own power. With subtle arguments she knows the best way to make us doubt our abilities, convince us of our inadequacies; and with the added poison of forgetfulness she keeps us her prisoner. The strength of the illusion she weaves is illustrated in the dream by the fact that when the dreamer finally makes every effort to break her chains, they fall away because they are so old. Only her feelings of failure, of being trapped, made her believe in the strength of these chains. But finally the desire for freedom is so strong that she is prepared to live in the world as her naked self: "If I have to walk naked down Main Street for the rest of my life, I don't care."

Accepting her own vulnerability, she is no longer the prisoner of the madman, no longer caught in the self-destructive patterns of which she was the victim. Vulnerability is frequently the price of freedom. Often we cover our vulnerability with self-destructive patterns, phobias, or addictions. A self-destructive pattern is a very effective way to securely enchain ourself, and possibly even destroy the potential for freedom, rather than having to live the terrible exposure of just being our naked self. We carefully find the weakest area of our character and at this point attack ourself. Sometimes our self-destruction is so successful that we never have to face the pain of our deepest vulnerability. In other instances the dynamics of defense are enough to distract us, and we remain unaware that the castle walls we are erecting become the walls of our own prison. Many times we lose the key of the castle gates, and remain trapped in our patterns long after any enemy has departed.

There are also individuals who are born with a developed sensitivity that is too painful to bear, particularly if they grow up in a family or environment which does not support or respect such sensitivity, or even attacks a sensitivity it does not understand. Spiritual wayfarers sometimes come into this world with a quality of sensitivity that belongs to their inborn relationship to God, a fine attunement to His ways, which has no echo in their outside world. Without an echo or container, the child does not understand the purpose of this inner attunement. Then a dynamic can develop in which she attacks her own sensitivity, rather than endure the pain of its being unrealized, its potential unlived. Thus that which is most precious, which belongs to the soul, is abused and wounded. Only later, when the wayfarer finds a spiritual group or teacher that values such sensitivity, can these wounds be exposed and healed. Gradually the wayfarer can reclaim her inner attunement and live its true purpose.

Our dreamer suffered not only from a collective feminine pain, but also from a devotional nature alien to our masculine culture. She had tried to make her way in a material culture that does not understand an inner attitude of surrender, and so became imprisoned and tortured by its maniacal head and her own patterns of victimization. But now she has found the key of her vulnerability, and the space in which she was imprisoned transforms from moldy tiles into polished white marble, "lit from the ground up." She has realized the light that comes from the feminine ground of her natural being, and walks through the archway, an ancient symbol of initiation. She does not care that she is not covered, no longer protected by the values of the collective or her own patterns of denial. She cares only for the freedom to be her true self.

THE POWER OF REMEMBRANCE

But how do we arrive at this moment of "breaking free?" When the dream was shared another woman wisely said that you have to wait until the right time. For how do you know that your own desire for freedom is not just another pattern of avoidance, of not facing and taking responsibility for your real situation and your role as victim? In the dreamer's own life this pattern of victimization had been played out in her inability to find a job that could financially support her and also allow her to express herself creatively as a textile designer. She had been well trained, but somehow in the masculine workplace of North America she never found a well-paying job as a textile designer that enabled her to live above the subsistence level. Then, after much inner and outer struggle, she found a job. This dream came the night after she had received the last pay check from her old job and the more substantial first pay check from her new job.

Such a transition cannot be forced or demanded. Slowly, patiently, the inner process develops, often one step back for every two steps forward. Gradually we build up the inner strength to make the break to consciousness and freedom. Like the sailing ship that has to wait for the right tide and winds to set out, one cannot make the inner and outer transition until the process is complete. But when the moment comes, it must be seized, just as, when the wind and tide are right, the ship must sail, or miss the opportunity. The wayfarer works diligently and patiently until the right moment. Then a situation will constellate, an opportunity occur, in which old patterns can be broken and a new quality of consciousness come into one's life.

How do we know that it is the right moment, and not just wishful thinking? Often we don't, and we make many false starts, many attempts to break the chains before they fall apart. But the wayfarer perseveres because this is not a journey for "brittle, easily-broken, glass-bottle people," but for serious men and women who have made an inner commitment to realize something within themselves. Patient and persevering, we struggle with ourselves, knowing that it is not the outer result that matters, but real inner change, the change that makes it possible for us to live more fully in the light of our real Self. In the words of Abû Sa'id, "Expectation must be eliminated from your affairs. If you wish your actions to become light for you, in your actions you must be devoid of desire."[6]

Patience and perseverance are necessary but not enough to counter the pull of unconsciousness. The dreamer could have stayed forever in the swimming pool, enchained by the past. We need the power to pull ourself free, to break the chains even if they just fall away at the moment of resolve. The unconscious covers us with forgetfulness and denies us our freedom, but the wayfarer has a more potent tool, the power of remembrance. The remembrance of God is the most simple and dynamic way to free ourself from any encumbrance. The unconscious has its poison but remembrance is an antidote to any poison but the need for God. Each moment of remembrance connects us to our divine nature, which in the words of the *Katha Upanishad* is "that boundless power, source of every power, manifesting itself as life, entering every heart."[7]

Remembrance of God reminds us that we belong only to Him, and slowly it infuses us with the taste of this freedom and the power to achieve it. Remembrance awakens the potency of our real nature, of the soul that bows down only before God. How can we be a victim to worldly circumstances when we are made in His image and belong to Him? If we belong to the Creator, how can we be caught in His creation? Only if He wills it, and then we surrender to His will. Surrender is not the same as subservience; surrendering to our destiny is very different from playing the part of a victim.

The remembrance of God energizes the deepest need of the soul, the need to free ourself from the bondage of this world and return Home, "back to the dwelling place of our desires." This need is itself a greater power than any pattern of conditioning, any pull of unconsciousness, because it carries the stamp of the Creator and His divine will. Abû Sa'id stresses the primacy of need in fulfilling the work of the soul:

> This is not a task that reaches fulfillment through words. Until you cut, blood will not flow. This task can only be brought to completion through need.
> There must be need! There must be need![8]

Remembrance and need are the most powerful tools of the mystic, because they connect us to His love for us and our love for Him. In this closed circle of love there is space for no other, for no patterns of denial or pull into forgetfulness. "He loves them and they love Him" is the most powerful dynamic in existence, for it is the axis of the world, the very framework of His creation.

Remembrance gives back to us our own power which belongs to the dignity of the Self. This is very different from the power of the ego which draws us into conflict and the grip of duality. The power of the Self *is* freedom, *is* love, *is* a light shining in the darkness of our forgetfulness and unknowing. The power of the Self carries a quality of consciousness that is not caught in duality, but is a direct connection to oneness. The simple act of remembering God brings into our life an energy that can unchain us. Each time we remember Him, the power of His presence increases, until we are able to live His freedom. The dreamer leaves the swimming pool as her own naked self, unadorned and vulnerable, but the whole environment has changed, is filled with a different light. She will slowly come to realize that the place of her imprisonment was also the place of her rebirth, that through her captivity she came to know the real nature of freedom.

Each time we cry from the depths of our despair He answers us, but we need to bring His answer into our life, we need to live His need for us—"Until you cut, blood will not flow." Gradually, slowly, almost imperceptibly, our remembrance incarnates the power of the soul, a power that carries the imprint of His will. This power then needs to be lived, not as some abstract idea, but lived in the blood, in the passion for what is true. Confronting our own darkness, we are prepared to be naked, to be bleeding, to be made conscious:

> We are like the night, earth's shadow.
> He is the sun: he splits open the night with a
> sword soaked in dawn.[9]

We have come to associate power with repression, and are thus often antagonistic towards power. Power suggests that someone imposes his will at the expense of another. But that is power that manifests through the ego, while the power of the Self creates both freedom and wholeness. This power is necessary in order to manifest and live our inner integrity, an integrity that is not in conflict or competition with anything else, but *is as it is*.

FREEDOM FROM THE COLLECTIVE

To live one's real self, to be naked in the world, requires power. First there is the power necessary to break free from the patterns of conditioning, and then there is the power needed to live this individuality in the world, in an environment that continually tries to pull us back into the collective. Collective pressures are strong and subversive, subversive in the way they subtly suggest that we should "fit in" and not cause the disturbance that results from living one's real individual nature. The collective is very threatened by individuality—not the individuality of ego-expression but the real individuality of the Self.

For most people, "to be oneself" actually means to live within the collective norms of what is allowed, or to rebel against these collective norms. And the rebel, who plays out the shadow of the collective, is as much trapped within the collective as anyone. Living one's true Self, one's innermost essence, is totally beyond the confines of the collective, beyond any conditioning. The true Self belongs only to God, who is absolute freedom. The freedom of the Self is not to do what one *wants*, but to do what one *is*. This threatens the very structure of the collective which depends for its survival and support mechanisms upon patterns of co-dependency, patterns which often cohere around collective values and shadow projections. For example, in North America the strongest collective value is the importance of money (people are valued by the amount of money they have), while poverty carries a shared shadow projection. A friend who grew up in a Puerto Rican community in New York once shared a very moving dream in which she was told that in the past it was acceptable to be poor, but no longer. This attitude that despises poverty is so limited compared to the freedom of spiritual life, as simply expressed in another friend's reassuring dream, "On this path we are allowed to have no money in the bank!" Another Western collective shadow is vagrancy, yet the one who lives a life of spiritual poverty is always a vagrant in this world. The Sufi may outwardly live a "normal" life in a house or apartment, but inwardly we have no home in this world, but, in the words of the Prophet, are "a traveller, a passer-by, with clothes and shoes full of dust ... for this is not home."

Living the freedom of one's spiritual essence requires courage, determination, and strength. The wayfarer is continually confronted by the values of the collective, by its pressures and insecurities, and needs energy in order not to be pulled back, not to be trapped again. But if it is difficult for an individual to stand alone against the collective, how much more difficult *to travel in the opposite direction* to the mass of humanity. Yet this is the way the lover must travel, inwardly turning away from this world, going upstream, back to the Beloved. Even with all our strength we would be swept along with the mass of humanity as it flows out into the world of forgetfulness. We need a power greater than our own self; we need the energy and container of a spiritual path to take us Home. The following dream images the power of the collective, and how the dreamer, together with fellow wayfarers in a simple container, is carried effortlessly in the opposite direction:

> I am in a wooden, box-like vehicle with a few other people. There are partitions between us, but otherwise it might be a large cart or wagon; how it is propelled is not shown. We are traveling down a passageway, a long, long tunnel, the end of which is not within sight in either direction.

We in the cart are going in a direction opposite to the mass of humanity, which is walking in a trance, making a strange intoning sound as it steps in unison. I have heard a sound like this dreadful, hypnotic, primitive sound in movie scores, at times when demon worship or primitive rites are going on. The throng of humanity is massed as far as the eye can see, and beyond, in both directions, as they push up against the cart we are in, this container or vehicle. And they move together in the direction opposite to the car's movement.

I am terribly, terribly glad I am in this container because it would be monumentally difficult to escape moving in the direction of this thronged mass moving together down the tunnel if one was on one's own, on foot. But for us in the vehicle it is effortless, for it just goes on. The mass pushes up against us, only because the tunnel is so frightfully crowded, but it doesn't impede the motion of the vehicle in the opposite direction.

Truly, they aren't paying any attention to us, don't even see us, for they are in a trance, intoning this strange, deep and terrible tone, and moving on, their eyes fixed and unseeing.

Hypnotized, drugged by the values of the collective and the veils of illusion, the great mass of humanity walks in a trance. Going in the opposite direction is a small group of wayfarers, effortlessly being taken to God by God. The path is His container, made with His power and love to take us back through the tunnel, back Home. The more we align ourself with the path, perform its practices and follow its teachings, the more we are contained and supported by its energy. The path gives us the power and protection that we need to make the most solitary journey. In the East the path is often imaged as a caravan of souls crossing the desert of this world. A traveler cannot cross the desert alone.

We have to make the supreme effort and yet everything is given; the path is effortless. We have to stand alone and yet are supported by the path, carried along by the caravan. We need power to discover and live our naked, individual self, yet the spiritual path takes us into the arena of oneness, in a state of vulnerability and helplessness. We are a part of humanity and yet travel in a different direction. They are drugged by the values of the collective, for example the illusion that happiness is dependent upon money, while we are drugged by the wine of the Beloved, the taste of oneness.

"ASK, AND IT SHALL BE GIVEN YOU."

The wayfarer has to find her inner strength and yet everything is given, by the path, by the teacher, by the Beloved. This appears to be a contradiction only if we think that the path is separate from the traveler. Seen with the eyes of duality, a seeker is attracted to a path, learns its practices, and is guided by its precepts. But the mystic knows the deeper truth, that the wayfarer and the path are one. "There is a mysterious substance within the heart of the wayfarer that is both the pilgrim and the path." The power of the path is the power within the heart of the wayfarer; the container of the path is the heart itself, a heart awakened and protected by divine love. Everything that is given to the wayfarer comes from the oneness within the heart.

We need our own power and we need the power of the path. We have to stand on our own feet and yet be supported by the path, by the caravan of souls. When the path is awakened within us, many contradictions are contained and also have to be lived, primary among them the contradiction of our own strength and our helplessness in His hands. We are awakened to our own need, and to the knowledge that only He can fulfill us, and yet we have to find the strength and power within us to walk the path and focus on the goal despite all the difficulties that we may encounter, difficulties that we confront both within us and in our environment.

Later we come to realize the oneness of the path, a oneness that includes all aspects of ourself, our strength and weakness, our need and the remedy to our need. Our awakening to the path is itself a response to a need—the soul's need to go Home. From the perspective of duality there is a need to which we seek the remedy. But from the perspective of oneness the need and the remedy are co-existent, just as a question and its answer are two sides of the same coin. The potential to answer a need is present within the need; the key to unlock the chains is within our enchainment.

This key that unlocks us is a conscious awareness of our need, of our captivity. The moment we become conscious of our need and offer it to Him, the answer is present, although it may appear hidden. Christ's words reflect this oneness:

> Ask, and it shall be given you, seek and ye shall find; knock and it shall be opened unto you.
>
> For every one that asketh receiveth; and he that seeketh findeth; and to him that knocketh it shall be opened.[10]

The answer to every need is present within the need. Our need to have power to free ourself from the collective attracts that power. The more conscious we become of our need, the closer we come to the power. Finally, when we fully acknowledge our need and offer it to God, the power is present. In the circle of oneness our need is His need, and when we ask Him He comes to know His own need and responds. The situation then attracts the qualities that are necessary.

Offering our need to God makes conscious our connection with the divine. We reconnect our consciousness with His consciousness, and from this connection we can draw the power we need. Only when we remain isolated within the ego, unable or unwilling to make this connection, do we appear cut off and impotent. Even then we remain within the oneness, but the consciousness of the ego is blind to this greater wholeness and sees only its separation and isolation. The ego only sees its unanswered need, and struggles against life, sometimes winning, sometimes losing, seeking success and dreading failure.

Consciousness is the key: to become conscious of our need and offer it to God. But we avoid consciousness because it carries pain and responsibility. Consciousness expelled us from the Garden of Eden, and it confronts us with the depth of our separation from our Beloved. To know the depth of our own need is also to know that *we* cannot answer it. Consciousness awakens us to our own weakness, and yet this consciousness also attracts to us the power and strength we require. The danger is to identify with the power when it is given, to forget that it is an attribute of our Beloved. The strength that comes is a part of us and yet is given in response to our need, for the work of coming closer to Him.

Yet many people are understandably reluctant to contact and live their power because they are aware, either consciously or unconsciously, of the corruptive nature of power, the danger of misusing power and of getting caught in the power dynamics of the ego. They are averse to taking the risk and the responsibility. It is even possible to carry memories from the distant past of having abused power and suffering the consequences. But ultimately, in order to incarnate our divine nature, we need power. We cannot avoid taking up the mantle of our inner strength. But we can also make use of our reluctance by keeping a close watch on our attitude and actions, to make sure we do not use this power for the purposes of the ego, in particular not to have influence over others. Fear is a great watchdog, together with the constant remembrance of Him to whom we belong.

Consciousness makes us aware of our need and enables us to ask Him, to call out and to be given to. And consciousness also enables us to take up our own responsibility, to be ever vigilant over the ego, over any possibility that we might inappropriately use the power that we are given. As much as we ask Him for strength, we can also ask that we be protected against any misuse of this strength. In the words of a Sioux prayer,

> I seek strength, not to be greater than
>   my brother,
> but to fight my greatest enemy—myself.
> Make me always ready to come to you
> with clean hands and straight eyes.

POWER & SPIRITUAL LIFE II
THE GREATER JIHÂD

Once I had been a slave: Lust was my master,
Lust then became my servant, I was free:
Leaving the haunts of men, I sought Thy Presence,
Lonely, I found in Thee my company.

Al-Ghazzâlî[1]

The power that is stored within the human being is beyond measure, because it belongs to the Self, our divine nature. This power does not belong to duality and the dynamics of the ego, as a friend realized in an experience of the Self: "I dreamed I was totally me. God dwells in me as me.... It's me—it's God—so terribly, shamelessly me. Just lowly me, and lowly me is all-powerful, but can't be bothered with power. Power over *what?* There's nothing to have power over." Power that has neither subject nor object is not limited, but carries the potency and pride of true being. This is the pride of the Self, which also contains the humility of the Self—we are proud to be His servant. The inner journey takes us into the depths of our own being where the primal power of the Self exists as undifferentiated energy. We need this energy for the work; we need the power of our natural being in order to be ourself and live true to this unconditioned self. But untamed, the instinctual world would swamp us with its raw power, just as it dominates us with its instinctual drives.

Consciousness is needed to contain and integrate this instinctual energy. Consciousness enables us to ask and be given to, and it is also necessary for the process of individuation, in which we enter the instinctual world, transform its energy, and then use this power for the work. In Zen Buddhism there is a series of illustrations with commentary called the "Ox-herding pictures," or "Bulls," which describes the search for and transformation of one's true nature, imaged as a bull. These illustrations begin with the search for the bull. Next its footprints are discovered. Then the bull is found, then caught, tamed, and then ridden, until, as the commentary describes it, "Mounting the bull, slowly I return homeward.... Riding the bull I reach home."[2] Finally, in the image of an empty circle, the bull and the rider are transcended, the source is reached. The last image is the old man returning to the world, and the commentary reads, "Barefoot and naked of breast, I mingle with the people of the world."[3]

Modern psychology interprets the bull as the energy of the Self, which is first experienced as a raw, instinctual energy that lies hidden beneath the layers of our conditioning. When this energy is undifferentiated, it manifests through the ego as the desires and instincts that pull us into life and keep us enchained in its unending cycle. The work of the wayfarer is to consciously connect with this primal self and to transform it with love, acceptance, and self-discipline, so that it reveals its higher nature. As the series of ox-herding pictures progresses, the color of the bull gradually changes from black to white, imaging the process of transmutation; in the final image of the bull only the tip of the tail remains black. Through this work of purification our instinctual power becomes changed so that it no longer drives us, but "takes us homeward." How this process happens is a great mystery—it is one of the wonders of the path.[4] But at times it is a battle as we connect with our primal energy, feel its power, and try to contain it within the heart. This is the battle with the *nafs* that the Prophet called *al-Jihâd al-akbar*, the Greatest Holy War against the lower soul (in contrast to the lesser *Jihâd*, the war against the unbeliever).

In each of us this war rages differently, but it is more of a conscious challenge for men. Women are naturally a part of the instinctual wholeness of life; they contain the divine creative process within their bodies. Irina Tweedie explains this difference in answer to the question "Is the spiritual training easier for men or for women?":

> The woman at birth receives in her spiritual or psychic centers the creative power of God. It is there, latent. It is always there. The man fabricates the creative power of God within his physical body, and this creative power of God manifests on the physical plane as seminal fluid in man for the sake of procreation, to have children. For men the training is to use this energy which manifests itself as sexual energy, to transmute it so to say. For this practices are necessary. The woman needs only one thing. She must get rid of attachments.
>
> So for us women spiritual life is easier than for men, but to renounce is more difficult than for men.[5]

Sexuality and instinctual energy are a part of the same life force manifesting within the human being.

On the lower level this force brings us into life and into the circle of procreation. When it is transmuted onto a higher level, this same energy takes us Home. A woman already exists in the center of her being and within her body contains the divine secret hidden in creation. A man has to make the labyrinthine journey back to this center and master the primal energies of the unconscious: he has to learn to ride on the back of the bull.

In earlier times man's confrontation with the primal, instinctual world was symbolized in Western mythology by the slaying of the dragon. This was the heroic task of the knight, who, once free from the chains of his instincts, could then be in service to his higher nature, Our Lady. Unfortunately the Western image of "slaying the dragon" suggests pure force and repression of one's instinctual self, in contrast to the Eastern image of "riding the bull homeward," which is mastery not *solely* through force, in the same way that a horse is not tamed through force alone, but through a *conscious* relationship. Our Western attitude towards our natural instinctual self has killed too many dragons, dangerously cutting us off from our own instinctual relationship to life.

The Eastern approach to the instinctual world gives us a more balanced model, in which consciousness and power work together to transform the primal self, revealing its higher qualities. But this does not deny the nature of the power dynamic in the struggle with one's primal nature, as the commentary on the "Bulls" describes in "Catching the Bull":

> I seize him with a terrific struggle,
> His great will and power are inexhaustible.[6]

But then in "Taming the Bull," the battle won, the bull reveals its higher, natural, gentle nature:

> The whip and rope are necessary,
> Else he might stray down some dusty road.
> Being well trained, he becomes naturally gentle.
> Then, unfettered, he obeys his master.[7]

The Sufi does not seek to repress his instincts or desires, but to master them, knowing that everything is a part of His oneness and needs to be respected as such. But the wayfarer also knows that everything needs to be in service. How can he be in service to his Lord if he is the slave of his lower nature? For example, the regular practice of meditation is important, but at the beginning this usually requires self-discipline as inertia or laziness stands in our way. Yet at the same time we should not become the slave of self-discipline, of always having to practice meditation at a certain hour. For a year I tried to wake up to meditate at four in the morning, because my teacher said that this was the best time, when there are the fewest thought-forms in the air. But as much as I tried to master my body, I would fall asleep, or just be too tired to meditate. So eventually I gave up, and then found a few years later that I naturally awoke before five, and could meditate without struggle.

If there is too much effort it is not spiritual. Sufism teaches the middle path, everything in moderation. Rather than rejecting the world, the path leads towards a state of inner poverty, "the poverty of the heart," in which the lover looks only towards the Beloved, knowing real fulfillment comes only from Him. The pleasures of the world can be enjoyed, but we don't run after them because we know the deepest pleasure of the inner relationship to Him. For example, sexuality can be blissful, but it should not rule us. The mystic knows that there is a greater bliss waiting within the heart, as the Sufi master Bhai Sahib describes from his own experience:

> When I was young with my first wife, I rarely had any intercourse with her. Every night I merged into my Revered Guru Maharaj. There can be no greater bliss imaginable than when two Souls are merging into one with love. Sometimes the body is also merged. How is it done? Well, the Soul pervades the body, you see, that's how it is done. The body partakes of it, is included in it by reflection, so to say. And no bliss in the world is greater than this: when you are One with your teacher.[8]

In this work, transformation does not happen just through fighting one's lower self, but also through focusing on the heart, on one's higher nature. The struggle is real as one's lower self tries to dominate, to turn our attention away from what is higher, to submerse us in the world of the instincts. But the wayfarer fights back with the sword of *Lâ ilâha* and the power of remembrance. The conscious awareness that "there is no God but God" (*Lâ ilâha illâ 'llâh*) is a work of struggle and self-discipline as we turn away from the world of illusion, *Lâ ilâha*, and turn towards what is real, *illâ 'llâh*. Turning our attention towards our Lord, from the many back to the one, protects us from the unconsciousness of our lower nature and its desires. If we look towards Him, remember Him in whatever act we perform, then everything is permeated by His presence. Remembrance of God is the most simple and powerful "whip and rope" we possess for training the bull.

The power of our instinctual nature is that it makes us forget, swamping our consciousness with un-differentiated energy. Raw sexuality and the greed for money are powerful forces that can easily dominate us. And each of us knows what it is like to be caught and blinded by a particular desire, so that we see nothing else. Suddenly we find ourself seduced, trapped by the thought-forms of having a more satisfying relationship or a newer car. The instinctual world throws its veils of illusion over our mind, pulling us into a hunger that can never be fully answered. The ego loves this tempting abyss of self-indulgence, just as a child loves to be fully indulged by her mother. The instinctual world *is* the Great Mother, and has her promise of total fulfillment, but it is a promise that carries the price of forgetfulness and a fulfillment that is never realized.

In this shimmering veil the ego can forget itself, forget the burden of responsibility and put down the light of consciousness. The Great Mother calls to us, tempts us, imprisons us. The *Jihâd* against the *nafs* is the struggle against the ego and its pull into un-consciousness, its desire only to fulfill its immediate impulse towards self-satisfaction. A very real battle rages within the wayfarer between the pull of the ego and the whole instinctual world on the one side, and on the other the heart's need to remember and to hold the light of this remembrance.

Often this power struggle may provoke us just to "kill the dragon" and repress our desires, deny any mode of self-satisfaction. Then we feel victorious, like the knights of old. We may even feel like a saint who has mastered his lower nature. But usually these desires, repressed into the unconscious, become more powerful, take on the guise and cunning of the dark feminine, and again seduce us. The unconscious knows the cracks in our armor, the weakest points of our character, and knows exactly how to tempt us. Following the path of moderation, we do not repress our desires; we acknowledge them but do not allow them to dominate us. Conscious awareness of our lower nature is a powerful safeguard against the seductive power of the unconscious.

We should also be aware of the danger of using power to dominate ourself. There is a great difference between taming the bull and dominating it. To dominate is to force your will upon another, even upon your instinctual self. This can lead to inflation and imbalance. What is dominated by power cannot take us home, but will always resist with resentment, with its own repressed will. Power must be balanced with love and compassion, compassion even for one's weakness, one's need for indulgence. Too much restriction also becomes sterile, as my teacher once told us laughingly: "Spiritual things can get boring. One needs some chocolate or a little bit of sin." Sufism teaches both moderation and laughter.

TRANSFORMATION AND FAILURE

Each according to our own nature fights the greater *Jihâd*, the war against the *nafs*. Possibly for men this struggle is more obvious, more self-apparent, though a woman also has to realize her natural power and learn the wisdom of self-mastery. A conscious relationship to her instinctual nature has to be claimed, which often means facing the guilt and shame that cover this primal power. Guilt is a powerful weapon which the Great Mother uses to keep us caught in unconscious patterns, and women are more susceptible to guilt than men (my teacher would say that a woman can feel guilty about almost anything!), while shame has for centuries been a means by which a masculine culture has kept the feminine veiled and separate from her own natural self, the beauty and potency of her real being.

A woman also has to be especially careful not to over-identify with her masculine power drive, which is what our culture values most highly. Although a masculine power drive may be very effective in the work-place, inwardly it easily cuts her off from her instinctual nature. An overemphasis on her masculine drive can evoke a woman's primal anger as she feels her wholeness and natural relationship to life violated. Yet at the same time the masculine qualities of creating boundaries and of perseverance, sticking to the goal in spite of everything, often need to be fostered.

Each wayfarer has differing masculine and feminine qualities that are reflected in his or her approach to the path.[9] Some people like the idea of a challenge, and gladly go into battle, while others are more reluctant heroes. Personally I have always been attracted to the challenge of the spiritual quest, of turning towards God in everything. Since I know that only He can give me what I need, that only He can answer my difficulties, my struggle is to contain everything with love and offer it to Him. Without looking for results, or even for answers, I try to focus on the heart and the energy within the heart. This focus can require great will power and effort, yet it is the love within the heart that is the real energy of transformation. Through focusing I try to take this energy into the problem, even into the depths of my instinctual self, and then let love do its work. I also use the *dhikr* as a way to untangle knots and transform difficulties. Repeating His name, I focus my inner concentration on a problem, on a psychological block, and feel the way the energy of remembrance frees and transforms.[10]

The spiritual warrior seeks to transform everything with the energy of love, which is the greatest power of transformation. Anger, resentment, bitterness, and the deep instinctual energy within the psyche can all be touched by love. The heart can contain everything, can work in the very depths of our being without being turned into stone by the dark feminine or torn to pieces by the wild energy of Dionysius. The heart is king, and all aspects of the psyche respect its authority. But I have personally found that one of the most difficult lessons of this heroic quest is to accept that there are inner and outer situations which I cannot change. As much as I seek to master myself, I have needed to learn that I am not the master. Even great love leaves certain situations unchanged, because the heart is His servant, and the will of God follows its own ways. In humility we accept and learn to live with our own failings and learn not to fall into the trap of the power principle which seeks to rule everything, to make everything perfect.

The Great Mother fights to keep us in her grip, to stop us with all her cunning and might from having access to our own instinctual power, for she knows that this power can give us our freedom. But everything is subservient to the will of God, and if it is His will that we come to Him, even the Great Mother will allow us what we need. We have to fight, fight our own lower nature, the ego, the shadow, and other aspects of our personality and psyche. We have to claim what is ours. But if it is His will, the opportunity is always present.

Our inner struggle and mastery of some aspects of our self give us the power we need for the journey. The bull gladly takes us Home, for in so doing it lives out its own highest potential. The more we are master of ourself, the more access we have to our own power, and the more we are able to use this energy for inner work. We need power to confront our personal shadow, the "dark side of our character," for example our cruelty or bitterness. We need even more power and strength for our family shadow, the skeletons which every family keeps carefully locked in its patterns of dependency. In order to bring these secrets out into the light of our own consciousness we have to fight the collective power of the family which wants to keep everything unconscious or blame the "problem" on one member of the family. If the wayfarer is to be free of the chains of a family dynamic, its shadows need to be accepted. But at the same time we must not force this consciousness on others, but allow other family members to remain in their familiar shadowlands. It is a dangerous ego-trip to think that others should share your consciousness.

Finally, the wayfarer has to confront the collective shadow of the race, for which great power and strength are needed. Each culture has its own shadow, some more visible than others. The shadow of the United States is very visible in its violence and its addiction to consumerism, and less visible in its treatment of the feminine. Again, just as the wayfarer does not seek to change her family, but just to free herself, we do not try to change the collective but only to change ourselves. Surrendering to His will, we know that all is in His hands, but in order to look to Him more fully and follow His will we need to be free of the restrictions created by any shadow dynamic or collective conditioning.

At each stage of the journey we are offered the power we need for the work we have to undertake. We are also given the consciousness we need in order to discriminate, for example to decide which desires to allow and with which desires we need to struggle. The difficulty is always to accept the power and the burden of conscious responsibility that it brings. The more power to which we have access, the more we are limited in our freedom of choice, and the more we have to live a life of duty. If we have access to only a little power, we cannot do much damage. But the more power we have, the greater the damage we could do if we used it for the ego, or worse, for our shadow-self. The boundary becomes so fine that one needs help either from the Higher Self or from a spiritual superior. My teacher said that "Big Brother" was watching everything she did, by which she meant that her teacher was always watching. And I know for myself that if I ever transgress a certain boundary, an inner presence, whether my Higher Self or my Sheikh, responds with absolute authority, an authority whose power is beyond measure. Knowing the power of my Sheikh, I am always in awe.

STILLING THE MIND

We need power to discover our hidden light and bring it to the surface. We need power to battle with the *nafs*, to transform our lower nature. We need power to master our emotions, so that the singleness of our quest is not swamped by moods or indiscriminate feelings. Although we need to acknowledge our feelings, allow our emotions space and expression, the wayfarer has always to be attentive to the danger of being distracted from the heart's deeper purpose. Sometimes we need strength to turn away from feelings that become narcissistic, emotions that are self-indulgent.

We also need power for the work of stilling the mind. The mind is the greatest master of illusion, known in the East as the "slayer of the Real." Learning to still the mind is a prerequisite for any spiritual path, because spiritual experiences take place beyond the mind. Initially spiritual experiences may overwhelm the mind, but there comes the time when the mystic cannot progress without being able to silence the mind, both in meditation and in waking life. How can one catch the divine hint if the mind is bombarding us with thoughts? How can one merge into oneness when caught in the duality of the mind?

The mind is a separate entity over which the wayfarer can gain mastery. But the mind does not like to give up its freedom, its influence over us. For most of our life it has held a dominant position, and our education process stresses its supremacy. Through academic study we can learn to train the mind, to use it for our own purposes, our profession or interests. But even in rigorous mental exercise the mind is still in a powerful position, guiding our attention in whatever direction it chooses. The wayfarer needs to turn her entire attention back to God, which means to break the stranglehold of the mind. The mind has to be "hammered into the heart," to surrender to the higher purpose of the soul, so that our attention is not caught in the veils of illusion and the conflicts of this world.

The mind can be controlled by the practice of the *dhikr*, in which the repetition of His name stops the mind from taking us on its meandering course. Often the mind thinks us, rather than our having control of our thinking process. How often are we caught in patterns or sequences of thought that are unnecessary and uncreative? How often does the mind capture us with desires which, when we look closely, have little substance or real interest to us? The *dhikr* gives us a method of focusing the mind on our deepest desire and thus freeing us from its captivity.

The *dhikr* requires practice and patience as we gradually alter a lifetime's thinking process. The *dhikr* also requires willpower, the will power needed to constantly bring our mind back to repeating His name. Without will power we would be unable to break the grip of the mind's stream of thoughts, to bring our attention back to the simple sacred phrase of our remembrance.

The mind, belonging to duality, loves to compare and contrast, loves conflict and argument. Avoid arguing with the mind, because the mind can subversively draw our attention into the most meaningful argument or discussion. Simply by turning our attention back to God, repeating His name, we can discipline the mind and teach it to surrender. And because the mind is master of the body, "if the mind is surrendered, the body is surrendered."[11] The surrender of the mind is an important step on the path.

A human being is made in the image of God, and is tremendously powerful. But we scatter ourself in countless directions and so become a slave to the world. Through controlling the mind we are able to become one-pointed and to focus ourself on the goal. Then our will is aligned with the will of God, and it is His will that we turn away from the world and back to Him. Turning from the many back to the one, we regain our divine nature and the power to live it. The *dhikr* works within the mind and the whole psyche, aligning us with Him whose name we call, until His name pierces through the veils of separation, uniting lover and Beloved.

The *dhikr* allows the mind to be busy repeating His name, but meditation requires the complete stilling of the mind, as Joe Miller expresses in his straightforward manner: "If you don't shut off the thoughts that you have running wild in your mind, you can't meditate and you can't be at peace with yourself."[12] In order to have real spiritual experiences we need to stop the thinking process, for it is the mind that cuts us off from love's oneness and the infinite ocean of nothingness. Going beyond the mind, we enter the inner dimension of the heart, the meeting place of lover and Beloved.

The will power needed for the *dhikr* is also necessary in meditation for the stilling of the mind. Practicing the *dhikr*, we focus on Him as we go about our outer life, while meditation requires a complete inner focus. The importance of total inner focus is expressed in a story about Bâyezîd Bistâmî and his teacher:

> Bâyezîd Bistâmî, sitting at the feet of his teacher, was suddenly asked, "Bâyezîd, fetch me that book from the window."
>
> "The window? Which window?" asked Bâyezîd.
>
> "Why," said the master, "you have been coming here all this time and did not see the window?"
>
> "No," replied Bâyezîd. "What have I to do with the window? When I am before you I close my eyes to everything else. I have not come to stare about."
>
> "Since that is so," said the teacher, "go back to Bestam. Your work is completed."[13]

Such an attitude of complete dedication to the work at hand is an inspiration for every wayfarer who knows how easily he is distracted both outwardly and inwardly. How often, as we sit in meditation, does our attention wander, to other people or to events past and future, before we catch ourself and have to bring our attention back to the present moment and our inner contemplation?

Different meditation practices use different methods of stilling the mind. The heart meditation practiced by some Naqshbandi Sufis uses the energy of love, as Irina Tweedie explains:

> We have to imagine that we are getting hold of every thought, every image and feeling, and drown them, merge them into the feeling of love.
>
> Every feeling, especially the feeling of love, is much more dynamic than the thinking pro-cess, so if one does it well, with the utmost concentration, all thoughts will disappear. Nothing will remain. The mind will be empty.
>
> It is a spiritual practice to control the mind, and also a useful exercise of will power.[14]

We so often have the experience of being love's victim, at the mercy of its coming or going, that we forget that love is also a stream of energy that comes from our own heart and can be focused and directed with will power. Just as we use the will power to turn our attention from the many thoughts of the mind to the one thought of His name, so we can use will power to silence the mind with love. Once love has been awakened within the heart, the lover can use it as a means to come closer to her Beloved, can fight the mind with the greatest power in the universe. The more we focus the light of our own love beyond the mind, the more we attract the light of His love, and when they come together the dualities of the mind disappear in the oneness of real love.

Through meditation we both control and surrender the mind. The mind itself can be frightened, as it stands on the borders of the unknown, of a reality into which it cannot pass. It will fight with all its cunning and power, but the will of the wayfarer is greater, because it is charged with His will. Slowly, gradually, over the years, the mind accepts that it is no longer master, and learns to surrender. In meditation the individual mind merges into the universal mind, and we are free of the burden of self.

Each day in meditation we still the mind to the best of our ability. Everything fluctuates and changes; there are good days and bad days, days when the mind is very active, other days when it slips into emptiness. There are also different levels of the mind. Initially the outer mind is active, giving us a stream of thoughts. Later, after practice, the inner mind comes to the fore, which has a different quality, nearer to pure consciousness. When the mind is totally still and empty one can experience this pure consciousness which is the witness (*shâhid*), a quality of awareness that watches without judgment or the duality of thought. Then in meditation this consciousness also goes, as one is lost in the beyond.

I have also had periods of meditation when there are thoughts but not the awareness that I am meditating. Then I have to become conscious that I am meditating in order to still the mind. Thoughts can come and go and yet in the center there is a place of emptiness, as a certain consciousness is absent.

Stilling the mind, we sit and wait. We create an empty space for our Beloved to come to us. Often we remain empty of His presence, resting in the dynamic silence that is within the heart. But sometimes He comes and takes us beyond ourself. The power of His love lifts us out of ourself into a different dimension. As we are brought into His presence, we begin to taste the Reality that lies beyond duality, the eternal emptiness that is the home of the mystic. Whatever effort we make, however much we discipline our mind, finally the mind cannot go beyond the mind, the ego cannot go beyond the ego. At His threshold our efforts become nothing; all our power fades away. With the infinite power of His presence He takes us to Him.

DIVINE QUALITIES AND RESPONSIBILITY

We need power on the path, power to confront the shadow and free us from our conditioning and the pull of the collective. We need the power to be ourself and to live our own divinity, to step from the grip of the ego into the arena of the soul, to follow the ways of love in a world that has forgotten Him. We need to find the power within us to transform our instinctual self and battle with the *nafs*. At each stage of the journey our efforts release the power we need for the next step. Struggling with our instinctual nature, we are able to master this "bull" and ride it homeward. With intense effort we direct our inner attention on the heart and the invisible goal, stopping our energy from being dispersed in so many conflicting directions. We use the power of remembrance to focus on the one, and thus bring the energy of His oneness into our life, into a world of seeming multiplicity.

Gradually we learn to master ourself and to use our potential for the purpose of the path. But at each stage there is an increased responsibility that we not use our power for the purposes of the ego. Free will becomes more and more aligned with duty, as our consciousness becomes the watchdog of our actions.

When we step from the stage of the ego onto the stage of the Self, when our life begins to be directed by this higher calling, we begin to attract the qualities that belong to the Self, His divine names and attributes. The energy and power of these qualities are many times greater than those of the ego's qualities. The ego supplies the energy we need for the work of the ego; the Self provides the divine energy we need for the work of the Self. The power accessible to the seeker increases dramatically when he has direct access to the divine, when His names and attributes begin to be incarnated. Through these qualities He is able to manifest Himself within His servant and within His creation; "God becomes the mirror in which the spiritual man contemplates his own reality and man in turn becomes the mirror in which God contemplates His Names and Qualities."[15]

"No one knows God but God," but through His qualities we come to know Him. The servant comes to know his Lord through experiencing His attributes within himself. We experience His majesty, His beauty, His mercy, His infinite grace, in the depths of our heart, in the very substance of our being. Although we know that we are other than He, we experience His imprint within us. As we walk along the path we each find certain qualities developing within us, qualities that specifically help us on our way. For one wayfarer the quality of compassion may begin to shine more brightly, while another may develop spiritual generosity, or yet another may be blessed with a clarity of consciousness.

These divine qualities which had been latent within the individual become infused with the energy of the Self, with His light, and belong not to the personal psychology of the wayfarer, but to the deeper purpose of the soul.

"Every being has his own appropriate mode of prayer and glorification," and our particular divine quality or qualities enables us to worship Him and manifest His glory in our own unique way, according to His will. While our personal psychology remains within the sphere of the ego, and often reminds us of our limitations and weaknesses, these divine qualities reflect the infinite dimension of our deeper nature. The more we turn from the ego towards the Self, the weaker the dominance of our personal psyche and the stronger the influence of His names. Finally the mystic who is lost in God loses his own name, and becomes like a signet ring that bears God's name: "The heart of the sheikh was considered a signet ring on which the divine names and attributes are imprinted."[16]

The divine attributes are given to the lover in trust, so that he can come to know His Lord and reflect His light into the world. Knowing that they are given in trust, the servant is always attentive to their right use, to reminding himself that they belong to His Lord. They are a responsibility that demands constant vigilance that we use them only for His work and never for the purposes of the ego. Always remembering that we have no other position than servanthood protects us from inflation, but "the travelers on the spiritual path are constantly faced with the danger of leaving servanthood and ascribing God's attributes to themselves. No one can consider himself immune from the divine deception."[17]

These qualities given to us in trust are both an honor and a burden. But by clinging to our state of servanthood we give our trust back to God, for "God commands you to deliver your trusts back to their owners" (Qur'an, 4:58). When the wayfarer offers His qualities back to Him, offers back to Him His power, then he "remains happy and burden-free in servanthood, which is his own possession."[18] First we take up the responsibility and burden of our divine nature and then we offer it back to Him. Knowing that everything belongs to our Lord, and that we are but His servant, frees us from the burden and responsibility we must embrace.

Not only His divine attributes but also inner mastery brings with it a tremendous responsibility. The one-pointed mind of the lover is aligned with the will of the Beloved. My teacher said that she had to be careful what she thought because it could come into being. But the sincere seeker is always guided and protected by the Higher Self and the inner presence of the teacher and the succession of superiors. These spiritual beings who are united with God look after us, and test us at each stage to see if we have the right attitude, to see the degree of our surrender. Bhai Sahib said to Irina Tweedie, "My people are tested with Fire and Spirit, and then sent out into the world, and never, never do they go wrong."[19] The further we go along the path, the more we are tested and the more the ego has to bow down and give up its autonomy. But the wayfarer remains always attentive to the deception of the ego.

The wayfarer under the protection of his sheikh is safeguarded from the dangers of inflation and the possible misuse of power. The power and authority of one's sheikh is absolute; there is nothing to be gained by argument or dissent. The ego may try to rebel, just as a two-year-old may kick in the arms of its parent. But with the love, authority, and power given by God, our superiors guide us on our way. And if the wayfarer does not accept this authority, does not inwardly bow down, then the power of the path is withdrawn, and the wayfarer will not progress any further. The masters of the path are the guardians of the grace of God, which is given for the work, for the purpose of drawing the wayfarer closer to Him and bringing His light into the world.

We have to make every effort, but without the power of the path and the grace of our sheikh we cannot progress. I once had an experience in which I was shown what happens when this grace is withdrawn, and for some days I walked in a colorless world, with no sense of inner direction, no joy in my footsteps. Then, just like a connection being switched back on, the grace, the energy of the path returned; again there was guidance and His light around me. I was shown quite simply that we are nothing without this energy, that the path, the whole life of the wayfarer are dependent upon His grace.

We need to discover and live our own power, and yet, as Rûmî writes,

> in a hundred thousand years you will not arrive at the first way station.... You imagined that you would accomplish this task through your own strength, activity, and effort. This is the Wont that I have established: expend everything you have in Our way. Then Our bounty will come to you ... then God's grace will take you in its arms.[20]

The lover knows that everything is dependent upon the will and love of the Beloved. We are in His hands, and only He can help us. Only His grace can lift us out of ourself and take us to Him, and only His light can guard us from the dangers of our own self.

This light and love are hidden within our own heart, where we have to find and then live them. His friends are the guardians of His grace and love in this world, the doorkeepers of love. To live centered within the heart is no easy task, because it means vulnerability as well as responsibility, responsibility not only to the burden of what we have been given, but also to the need of the moment, the need of the Self. To live the ways of love is to follow the path of Khidr, and although it is the path of the highest ethics, nothing is written down. The ways of God cannot be written in the words of this world. His hint is quicker than lightning, faster than the mind. Only a mind surrendered to His will, a mind hammered into the heart, can catch His hint, and only one burnt in love will dare to live it.

Those who have traveled this far along the path are entrusted with helping in the work of their Beloved. They are the Friends of God, who are protected in their tasks by "the lights of protection." The ninth-century Sufi al-Hakîm at-Tirmidhî describes how, although these Friends of God still possess their lower nature, they are protected from their "carnal soul" by the light of Friends higher in rank, those who have gone before them:

> They [God's chosen few and His advisors to mankind] allot a portion of the light to these Friends, and this light guards over them as long as they are engaged in these tasks. Then whenever any fault from the carnal soul emerges in their breast, the light's rays shine forth in the person's breast and conceal from the heart and the carnal soul what has

> emerged, and it is rendered null and void. And
> so the person undertakes his task, proceeding
> straight ahead and without turning his
> attention to anyone else. Then he returns
> untarnished to his position and his station.[21]

Walking in this world according to His ways, we are given what we need to accomplish His work, to learn to love Him, to come near to Him, and to bring His love into the world. Our power and our humility are our own protection, and once our power is infused with His light and love, and the light of His Friends, it protects His work. In the circle of oneness everything is given, everything is dependent upon both the lover and the Beloved. Our work is to look to Him, honor what He has given us, and use it for His work. He needs us to come closer to Him and has given us the means to travel this infinite road. His oneness is always present, but we need power and devotion to remember it, and in this remembrance to live it.

The more we step into the circle of the heart, the more we realize that everything comes from Him, and yet the greater becomes our own responsibility to live it. We live His oneness through surrender, a surrender in which our very essence as well as our attributes are offered and accepted and in this acceptance transformed. Mystical oneness is not an abstract idea, but a living reality in which we incarnate our duty to Him and His love for His servant. This interplay of oneness and duality cannot be understood by the mind, because from within oneness duality takes on a different texture. Merged in God, we remain His servant, ever attentive to His needs which are impressed into our own heart.

THE ABYSS OF
ABANDONMENT

*The way of love is not
a subtle argument.*

*The door there
is devastation.*

*Birds make great sky-circles
of their freedom.
How do they learn it?*

*They fall, and falling,
they're given wings.*

Rûmî[1]

PREPARATION

"The path," writes Rûmî, "is not for brittle, easily-broken, glass-bottle people. The soul is tested here by sheer terror."[2] What is this terror that awaits the wayfarer? What are the depths of despair that we are forced to confront? Can we be prepared, or is the only preparation our desire to face whatever is given, to surrender to the path's devastation?

Every traveler has to journey within, to cross the boundaries into the unconscious, into the unknown inner world which is the home of the shadow. Here we encounter our own darkness, our rejected and repressed selves, the cruelty, pain, and poison as well as the positive qualities, lurking in the depths. In these shadowlands we are tested. Do we have the humility and strength to accept what has been rejected, not only by ourself, but by our families and even by our whole culture? All the hunger, violence, and despair, the wounds that we so carefully cover up, come to meet us; and we are forced to witness the disintegration of our personality, "what we like to think we are," in the face of what we discover we are.

The work on the shadow is a painful, demanding process, but one that is a necessary preparation for the mystical path. Through our loving and accepting what we find in the depths, our whole psychic structure is transformed, lead is turned into gold, and the energy that has been locked in the depths is released. The energy that has been stored in the shadow is needed for the journey; we need the power of our own repressed self to cross into the beyond. This work in the darkness frees us from our personal and collective ego-identity, giving us a glimpse of the primal wholeness of the Self.

THE JOURNEY TO THE ABYSS

The confrontation with the shadow opens the doorway into the mysterious depths of our own being, into a dimension beyond our conscious understanding. But the path then takes us further, deeper, and there comes the time when we confront an abyss so terrifying that our personal darkness seemed like a safe refuge. The following dream tells of the journey to this abyss, to this place where being is confronted by the infinite emptiness of non-being. Every mystic comes to this edge, beyond which only the brave and foolhardy dare pass.

I am on board a tall ship in remote antiquity. The sails are being lowered as we enter the harbor of an important city. There is lots of activity in the harbor and on the large nearby plaza. The ships are busily unloading; on the plaza people are coming and going, buying and selling in a large open market. Purposefully, but without hurry, I land with a group of people, about forty, of whom I am the leader. People seem to look up to me. The purpose of our coming here is to meet Moses, who will then be our leader.

We start looking for Moses. We wait, we ask questions. I send emissaries all over the city, but no one sees him; he hasn't come yet. So we wait, and wait, in the sun and in the shade. In vain. Finally I decide that he has probably gone already, and that we will find him somewhere on the mountain. So I gather the group, which somehow has become smaller. And we start going up the mountain. It is a long, arduous climb; we obviously need endurance, not agility, for it is not hair-raising, but it is tiring, on and on, up and up.

There is no Moses in sight. We are now very high, and it is becoming misty, foggy, disquieting. Some of us are grumbling, some give up. The group gets smaller and smaller and becomes ultimately a handful, maybe seven. Finally we rest on the top, the end of the path.

> Here the mountain seems to have been slashed
> with a gigantic axe.... In front of us is a deep
> cliff, below a huge, infinite chasm; above, the
> immense sky, a bit hazy; behind, the endless
> slope, swallowed by the fog. And no Moses.
> He didn't come after all, he is nowhere, he
> stood us up. We have no place to go, we don't
> know what to do. We feel lost, abandoned,
> dreadfully alone, and I even more so, for I feel
> responsible for this ominous situation.

The dream begins with a ship arriving in a port.
The dreamer is the leader of a group of forty people,
who disembark and begin looking for Moses. The first
stage of the journey has been completed, and the
search begins in earnest. Forty is the traditional number
of the quest; forty days is the period of a traditional Sufi
retreat (*chilla*), while Moses led the Jewish people
for forty years in the wilderness before reaching the
Promised Land. Our dreamer is searching for Moses,
for this inner figure who will free him from the
captivity of the ego and the world of the *nafs*.

The bustle of the port, the coming and going,
echoes the initial activity of the quest. The inner
journey often bursts into consciousness with a feeling
of excitement and activity. You arrive at the port of
your own search and are surrounded by all the possibilities of your longing. In the present "new age"
culture, spiritual life is visible in the marketplace; there
are books to read, workshops and lectures to attend.
Often seekers become confused by all this activity,
caught in the surface phenomena of the quest. They
read too many books, attend too many workshops,
and are distracted from going deeper beneath the
surface. But our dreamer is focused in his search

for Moses, for the inner guide who will lead him to freedom.

Up till now the "I" in the dream, the dream-ego, has been the leader. It often appears that we begin the quest with this sense of purpose and direction. Gathering aspects of our self together, the forty travelers, we set off in search of a goal, enlightenment, spiritual fulfillment, Truth. The deeper reality, that the ego can not know the object of this quest, does not surface until later. The spiritual path takes us into the realm of oneness, where the ego, whose very nature is to be separate, cannot enter. But at the beginning of the journey back to God the seeker is looking for something, has some conscious sense of direction. The lover has an object for her longing—her Beloved. The duality of lover and Beloved is fixed in her consciousness, is stamped into the pain of separation. The path to oneness, to the knowledge of love, means that this duality will dissolve, our sense of a separate self will die. And then the path leads even further, from the oneness of true being into the nothingness of His non-existence. But the lover traveling inward into this infinite beyond initially looks towards a distant horizon, towards an image of her Beloved.

He for whom we search is the very center of our being, but like the fishes who search for water we need to make the journey, and one of the first steps is to find a guide, to find the wisdom that will take us there. Amidst all the initial activity and bustle of the journey, our dreamer is looking for Moses, for his guide. He searches everywhere, but there is no sign of Moses. The paradox of the mystical journey is always present within this dream, the suggestion that "there is no dervish, or if there is a dervish, that dervish is not there."[3] Yet this is wisely hidden from the dreamer, who asks questions, sends out emissaries. But no one has seen Moses; he hasn't come yet. "So we wait and wait, in the sun and in the shade."

We are so conditioned that there must be an object to our search that we have to look, to ask questions. But there is no Moses, no "other" who will take us by the hand and guide us. At the beginning we may think that a spiritual teacher can fulfill this task. But all a guide can do is open us to the depths of our longing and point us to the Beloved. In Rûmî's words,

> The guide will take your falcon's hood off.
> Love is the falconer, your king.[4]

When Irina Tweedie said to her sheikh that he could give her God, Bhai Sahib just laughed at the ridiculousness of the idea. Only He can reveal Himself in the hearts of those who love Him.

QUALITIES AND ATTRIBUTES

Eventually the dreamer thinks that Moses may have gone ahead, be already on the mountain. So he sets off up the mountain with his group, which has grown smaller. During the course of this dream-journey the group of travelers becomes smaller and smaller, until finally only about seven arrive at the mountain top. In *The Conference of the Birds* 'Attâr also portrays a diminishing number of birds in the quest for the Simurgh. At the outset many birds make their excuses: the duck says that she is too timid, the partridge is too attached to precious stones, the heron's love is entirely for the sea, while the owl who lives in melancholy among ruins, hoping to find buried treasure, says that love for the Simurgh is but a childish story.

As the journey progresses, other birds fall away. Many people who begin the search lack the commitment or perseverance to continue along this narrow path, are distracted or discouraged. At each turn and twist of the path stragglers fall behind, to be waylaid by insecurities, doubts, desires, or other weaknesses. Christ's words, "Many are called but few are chosen," add a poignancy to this testing, suggesting that it is also the will of God which separates those whose commitment will drag them to the bitter end from those who will be drawn back into the ego, still caught in the veils of illusion.

But in the symbolism of a dream the different figures are usually read as aspects of the dreamer. If we interpret the dream in this way, what does it mean that the forty travelers become only a handful? At the beginning of the journey when we embrace spiritual life with all our enthusiasm, many different inner qualities and character-istics are included. Our intellect may be captivated by the brilliance of spiritual literature, our love of music enthralled by the wonder of spiritual music, whether the cantatas of Bach or the piercing wail of the reed flute. Maybe our ambition is attracted by the notion of a tremendous challenge and the possibility of achieving realization, while a sense of determination also finds a task in which it is needed. Our need for friendship may be met by the warmth of a spiritual group, while a longing to surrender may find its place at the feet of a teacher.

We each have many different qualities which try to include themselves in the path. Generosity and kindness, as well as pride and jealousy come to the surface, wanting to be included. Who has not felt jealous about another's spiritual progress, or been flattered by her own experiences? In the initial stages of the journey these qualities are lived and accepted— to deny or repress them would be psychologically harmful. But soon the sword of discrimination is needed to separate those qualities that belong to the ego and bind us to the *nafs* from those qualities which can free us and take us Home.

In this work of discrimination we should not judge by appearances, because qualities that seem spiritual may be deceptive. We may discover that kindness is just a cover for weakness, for avoiding stating and living our own truth. Or we may find that a quality of pride is needed, the pride that bows down before nobody but God. And is our love of beauty an attachment to *maya*, or is it that we see His face reflected in His world? Do we love to dance because our body can express His movement, or is it an attachment to the world of the senses? There are no rules for this work of discrimination except the simple practice of sincerity and self-awareness. Each wayfarer has a unique combination of qualities, some of which belong to the work of the soul, and some of which are only an obstacle.

Through prayer and insight we come to know the few qualities that carry His stamp and will take us back to Him. Gradually we come to recognize that these qualities have a different and deeper resonance than those parts of our character that belong only to the ego. We may also discover that qualities which we thought a weakness or psychological problem are the very qualities the soul needs, and that they were only a problem when viewed from the perspective of the ego or the external world. It took me many years to realize that my inability to fully relate to others came from an imprint in which my face had been turned towards Him, while the pride which had supported me for many years, giving me a strong sense of identity, had to be broken down and thrown aside.

The qualities that carry His stamp belong to the soul and do not come from our background or childhood. They often carry an intensity that makes them difficult in daily life, and can be experienced as a social or psychological liability until we live them in relationship to the path. They are too powerful for the ego, and have a purpose different from its constricted goals. This is why they may distort our personality, even our psychological make-up, until we live them for the purpose to which they belong. Slowly, as we journey homeward, these qualities reveal their potency, and we realize that we cannot change or adapt them, because they are made to change us. They are stronger than our ego, more powerful than our personal psychology, and we need them to cross into the beyond. As the path tears us apart, these qualities remake us; they forge into our consciousness His name with which they are engraved. They are the tools with which the blacksmith of our soul bends us into the shape which He wills, the shape engraved in the book of our own destiny.

PATIENCE AND PERSEVERANCE

While we each have individual qualities that define the unique way the path will remake us, there are also qualities that can help every wayfarer. As our dreamer makes his journey up the mountain, an archetypal symbol of spiritual ascent, he finds that he needs endurance, not agility, on this long, arduous climb. Endurance and perseverance are a necessity for the wayfarer committed to the slow, painstaking work of inner purification, the struggle with the *nafs*, the polishing the mirror of the heart.

Day after day, week after week, year after year, we struggle to remember God, to bring His imprint into our daily life. The light of our remembrance brings into consciousness the darkness of the shadow, the addictions of our lower nature. With love, devotion, and endurance we stick to the struggle with our lower nature, often seeming to take one step back for every two steps forward. Many times, during these days, the Beloved seems to have disappeared, leaving us alone with our darkness and our longing. Each step appears to be made solely through our own effort, for we are not yet conscious of His grace which is helping us, guiding us, supporting us. Without endurance we would falter, give in to our despair and frailty.

These are not dramatic challenges that face us, challenges that would arouse adrenaline and the pride of a great struggle. Rather we are faced with our own pettiness, with our insecurities, with our doubts. We are more aware of how often we forget Him, how often the *dhikr* slips from our mind, how we are mired in worldly activities. The daily events of our outer life absorb almost all our attention. Mundane difficulties and problems besiege us.

Turning our attention from the world back to our Beloved, freeing ourself from the grip of the *nafs* and accepting our own humanness, is a long, arduous journey during which many seekers abandon the quest, seeking something more stimulating, more immediately fulfilling. We need the attribute of patience, as the ninth-century Sufi al-Hakîm at-Tirmidhî clearly states:

> God said, "These shall be rewarded with the upper-floor chamber because they have been patient." Now the person who is patient de-

spite his character traits, his manner and defects, is the person whose heart God fills with knowledge of Himself, and God expands his breast with His light and thereby bestows life on his heart. Moreover, patience consists of persevering at something and remaining firm in it.[5]

Patience and perseverance belong together, giving us the forbearance and firmness necessary to stick to the path despite our weaknesses. We cannot reject our weaknesses, our shadow qualities, because that would just give them more power in the unconscious. Acknowledging that they are a part of our character, we keep them from dominating or distracting us. At the same time, too much attention to struggling with our weaknesses, trying to improve ourself, poses the danger of diverting us from the primary purpose of our inner work. The desire for self-perfection is a trap many wayfarers have to avoid.

With discrimination we learn to walk the middle path, knowing that only He is perfect. With patience and perseverance we stay true to our innermost desire, as is illustrated in a story told by al-Junayd:

> I met one of the young seekers in the desert under an acacia tree and asked him what made him sit there. He replied, "I am looking for something." Then I passed on and left him where he was. When I returned from the pilgrimage, I found he had moved to a spot closer to the tree. I asked, "Why are you sitting here?" He answered, "I found what I had been looking for in this place, so I stuck to it." I do not know which was more noble, his

persistence in seeking his state or his perseverance in staying at the place where he attained
his desire.[6]

CONFUSION AND DESOLATION

The dreamer climbs higher and higher up the mountain, and still no Moses is in sight. Instead, on the
mountain "it is becoming misty, foggy, disquieting."
Expecting to find the guide, we find our own unsureness;
expecting to find clarity, we find confusion. The
mystical path is not for those who need a clear sense
of direction, but for wayfarers who are able to live
amidst contradictions, in the misty landscape beyond
reason's boundaries.

To enter this landscape is to encounter a dimension
of contradictions. Wayfarers who expected to find something will be disappointed, for nothing is defined; there
is nothing of substance. The mind is left in confusion; the
ego stands at the brink of an abyss. Up till now the path
was defined by our effort, by the work of purification, the
slow arduous climb up the mountain. Whatever the
difficulties of our inner struggle, at least they carried a
purpose, a definite goal. We knew that we were improv-
ing ourself, polishing the mirror of the heart. But now the
wayfarer has come to the end of the path, of the
purposeful search. Moses is not here; there is no way
forward, and the way back is swallowed by the fog.

What is the meaning of this misty landscape? What
is this abyss that awaits the traveler, this "infinite
chasm"? How is he to proceed? This is the place where
wayfarers expecting spiritual results or inner transformation have to surrender this baggage. This is the
place where the faint-hearted hold back. There is no

way forward. There is no way. There is only an abyss and the feeling of abandonment. In this ominous landscape every traveler is lost and desolate.

We come to realize that we have been deceived by the notion of the journey, by the idea of a goal. All the books and teachings that pointed out the way, that encouraged and helped us, did not prepare us for this. The bleakness is beyond description, the desolation terrible. Here there can be no confrontation, no struggle, because there is nothing tangible. Suddenly we come to realize the immensity of the task, and that our mind, our consciousness, our self cannot begin to comprehend what we have undertaken. In the port and on the mountain there was a purpose; now there is just swirling fog and an endless chasm.

This is the abyss of abandonment to which every wayfarer arrives, which Christ encountered when he cried on the cross, "*Eli, Eli lama sabachthani?* My God, my God, why hast thou forsaken me?"[7] Every fiber of our being cries out against accepting this abandonment, living this desolation. Existence is confronted by non-existence, form by formlessness. Our very existence is defined by form, by an identity, by a sense of who we are. Now each atom of our identity, even our spiritual identity, pulls back from the abyss. How can we give ourself to this undefined emptiness, where even our notion of God does not exist? In meditation we may have learned to surrender to what is beyond the mind, but this chasm confronts our whole life, our whole being.

The meaning of this chasm is that here all concepts, all identity must be left behind. *There is nothing to hold onto,* not even the notion of spiritual progress, or a loving and caring God. In the misty landscape at the edge of this chasm we have to leave behind that which is most precious. This is why the feeling of abandonment is so intense. One friend was suddenly confronted in a dream by the realization that she had to give up the desire to be loved. She was astonished, because she had always thought that the path would fulfill this need, that she would experience being loved. She was terrified at the notion of losing this deepest dream of being fulfilled. She thought spiritual life was about getting something, and an instinctual fear gripped her whole self when she realized what had to be given up. One can hear the saying "Everything has to go" ten thousand times without fully realizing its implications. But in the words of Lao Tzu,

> When the ancient Masters said,
> "If you want to be given everything
> give up everything,"
> they weren't using empty phrases.[8]

Another friend had a deep and ancient connection with her teacher, a connection of great love and devotion. Her love and respect for her teacher were at the very core of her being; this was the substance of her spiritual life. And her teacher let her down, proved inadequate, made mistakes. The devastation caused by this betrayal destroyed her. How could the path be real when the teacher had failed, had not understood the depth and meaning of her devotion and love, had mistaken it for attachment? How could she reconcile what had happened with her belief in the path?

> In the slaughterhouse of love, they kill
> only the best, none of the weak or deformed.[9]

Those who belong only to Him have to experience a desolation beyond any imagining.

We each have our deepest attachment or belief system. We want to be loved, to have a purpose in life, to find spiritual truth. We believe in justice, in *karma*, in a caring God, in a perfect teacher. This attachment or belief lies at the very center of our identity, and till now has been a great support on the path. Our journey up the mountain freed us from many attachments, outer as well as inner, and from many collective beliefs. No longer dominated by our lower nature, by shadow dynamics, selfish motivations or the patterns of the collective, we still cling to the support of our innermost belief. Usually it belongs to our spiritual identity, our sense of ourself as a seeker. Now it too has to be left behind. Our whole identity, even our spiritual identity, has to crumble. We need to be totally unsupported.

'Attâr tells a story of a venerable sheikh with many disciples who falls in love with a Christian girl. Sheikh Sam'an is in Mecca when he has a dream of bowing before an idol in Rome. This dream so troubles him that, together with his disciples, he sets out for Rome, where, one day, he sees a Christian girl whose beauty is like the sun in splendor. The sheikh's heart is lost to her beauty; he gives up his will to love's passion. His disciples are horrified and try to reason with him, but he refuses to listen:

> One urged him to repent; he said: "I do,
> Of all I was, all that belonged thereto."[10]

His disciples, realizing that he has lost his beliefs, and that their words have no effect, leave him. The Christian girl, seeing this old man so much in love, ridicules him, saying that he needs a shroud rather than her. But for the sheikh age means nothing; only his love for her matters.

The girl then says that if he wants to prove his love he has to drink wine (which is forbidden in Islam), and wash his hands of Islam. Once the sheikh drinks the wine he loses his spiritual knowledge; the Qur'an he knew by heart is washed from his mind. All that remains is his desire for her:

> Beside himself with love and drink he cried:
> "Command me now; whatever you decide
> I will perform. I spurned idolatry
> When sober, but your beauty is to me
> An idol for whose sake I'll gladly burn
> My faith's Koran." "Now you begin to learn,
> Now you are mine, dear sheikh," she said....[11]

The sheikh burns his dervish cloak and becomes a Christian. Despite the fact that he is an old man the girl begins to feel love for him, but to try his love further she insists that if she is to be with him he must look after her herd of pigs for a year. Without protest the sheikh agrees and becomes her swineherd. Love has taken him to this abyss, this depth of degradation. He has lost his beliefs, his honor, and he does not even have his beloved.

Love knows no limits. The sheikh loses all sense of self, all identity, and receives only grief:

> After so many years of true belief,
> A young girl brought this learned sheikh to grief.
> He said: "This dervish has been well betrayed;
> The agent was mere passion for a maid....
> May no one pass through wretchedness like mine!

Love ruins one like me, and black disgrace
Now stares a once-loved dervish in the face...."[12]

His former disciples, horrified at what has befallen
their revered sheikh, return to Mecca. But before leaving for Mecca one disciple comes to ask the sheikh
what has happened. The sheikh replies, "That faith was
conquered by insane despair." This disciple does not
abandon his sheikh, but prays for him until his prayer
is answered by the Prophet. The Prophet says that
between God and the sheikh there has been for a long
time a black speck; that speck has now been cleansed
and the sheikh is free.

In 'Attâr's story the disciple and his companions
rush to where the sheikh is keeping the pigs. The
sheikh, like one illumined, has already cast aside his
Christian clothes and the knowledge of God's law has
returned to him. The girl too receives illumination, and
becomes a disciple of the sheikh, but only briefly,
because, just as she embraces the search for Truth, she
dies: "She was a drop returned to Truth's great sea."

THE ABYSS OF FORGETFULNESS

Those who give themselves to the path of love are
each taken to the abyss where their old self must
be abandoned. Every identity, every belief, however
spiritual, is a limitation. In the words of Bhai Sahib, "You
cannot go to a high state when you stick to a belief."[13]
To step out into the infinite emptiness we need to
leave behind all limitations, all definitions of self
or purpose. This is the wisdom of spiritual poverty,
"having nothing and wanting nothing." But the terror
of the abyss comes from the desolation and destruction

that create this poverty, as what is most central to our sense of self is torn away. A friend had a dream in which every fiber of her heart was torn out except one fiber, the one string the Beloved would play.

This experience of destruction, of being torn apart, is often accompanied by the feeling of betrayal. To betray a human being in the core of his or her beliefs, in the very fabric of what he or she knows to be right, will destroy these beliefs. If we know that our Beloved is just, and He throws us into injustice after injustice, where do we turn? If we love our teacher, and this love is turned against us, is rejected, is misunderstood, where do we stand? We are betrayed in the very core of our being, again and again, until there is nothing left to betray, until we too have been made empty, until absolute poverty is our only friend.

The lover's journey is terrible because it takes us into the realm of what is absolute. Because He is without limits, there are no limits to the torture He gives to those who need to come close to Him. From when I first stepped through her door, my fear of my teacher was that I knew she would do anything for the sake of the Truth. I was always held entranced by the story her teacher told of the young man who was beaten to death by his sheikh, with the man's family looking on. The young man loved his sheikh, and just sat smiling at him as the sheikh used his stick and then a piece of wood to beat him until "one could not recognize who it was—nothing was there, just a mass of broken bones ... flesh and blood were everywhere. Then [the sheikh] stopped and said to the relatives of the boy: 'What is this? Am I not at liberty to do as I like?' 'Yes,' they said, 'we belong to you for life or death; you can do with us what you like.'" The sheikh went inside.

Later he came out and "pointing to the mass of broken flesh ... said, ... 'Get up!' And the boy got up and was whole, and not a scar was seen on him. And he was told by his Teacher that from now on he is a *Wali* [saint]."[14]

This story stamped into my being the intensity and absolute nature of the path, both in the treatment of the boy and in the surrender of his family who just watched, for they belonged to the sheikh "for life or death." The Beloved is our executioner, our torturer, our destroyer. The abyss is the emptiness that is at the core of our being, the essence of our love for Him. Longing drags us to the edge of this abyss and love throws us over. And the paradoxical nature of the path makes sure that the abyss appears in the way we least expect, the opposite of what we are prepared to encounter. For the woman who had to give up the desire to be loved, this was so unexpected that even as she told the dream she did not believe it—anything but that!

On my own journey this abyss was always present, though for years I struggled, not wanting to understand its real nature. The world into which I was born was for me empty and desolate beyond belief. For the years of my childhood I repressed this feeling, held it down with will power and denial. But soon after I met my teacher feelings of terrible abandonment began to surface, anger at being born, resentment at the emptiness of the middle-class environment of my upbringing. Nowhere in it was there any semblance of spirituality. We went to church, sang hymns and read the Bible, but His presence was not recognized; His love was hidden. The agony of my soul's sense of abandonment was deep and terrible. When it surfaced I felt the betrayal. How could He whom I love and adore, to whom I belong, send me into such desolation, into the wilderness of a world that did not know Him?

The abyss was all around me; it was the substance of my childhood. I did not know it then. I just experienced the terrible bleakness and believed it was life. There was no echo to my soul's knowledge that the purpose of life is to praise Him and come to know Him. The path brought this pain into consciousness, made me know the depth of the betrayal. He whom I love sent me into a world without Him. How could He do this, how could He separate me from His friends who love Him? How could He hide His face so much that I did not even know He existed?

For twenty years I wandered in this absolute wilderness until I met my teacher and the family of friends. Over the next twenty years I slowly became conscious that looking to Him, loving Him, praising Him, dissolving in His emptiness are all that give substance to my life. And for so many years I was denied it, almost to the point of madness. Why? Why was I not brought up in a family of His friends, of those who know and love Him? Why did He abandon me into the company of those who have forgotten Him?

Slowly I have come to realize that my soul carried a certain spiritual arrogance, an arrogance that came from lifetimes of spiritual seclusion and a rejection of ordinary life. This arrogance had to be beaten out of me, and what simpler way than to throw me into a wilderness without Him? I had to relearn the grace of being taken into His presence, of being allowed close to Him. What I have to offer is nothing. I have no value—He can dispose of me as He wills. In His eyes we are all equal, and only His glance gives us meaning.

I was born into a world in which there was no remembrance. No one looked towards Him. Everyone was busy with worldly activities. I felt so abandoned, so rejected, so desolate. As soon as I found my teacher I turned my back on my family, my parents, my brothers and sisters—I could not bear to accept that pain. I have come to realize that at the core of my being is the knowledge that I belong to God—this alone is what gives meaning and sustenance to life. And slowly I realize that I had to lose that belief—I had to forget that I know Him. I had to experience a world without Him, taste the terrible abyss of abandonment.

Of course He gave back what He took away, but the belief returns in a different way. We do not claim it for our own; we know that it belongs to Him, and is given back by Him, as He wills. The core of our being is not held by this belief, only by Him. And still I wonder at the mystery of His forgetting Himself.

The world is permeated with His knowledge of Himself, but we do not know it. Each atom, every leaf sings His praises, and we do not hear it. Every creature, every flower, every cell is imprinted with His name, and we do not see it. Our ignorance, our forgetting, is what creates this world of illusion. When we remember Him, we are able to see His face in His creation. When we forget Him, then this world becomes "a tale told by an idiot, full of sound and fury, signifying nothing." When I sense the desolation of a world without Him a terror fills me, a black hole from which there seems no escape. The abyss is still present within me, a constant reminder of how much I am dependent upon Him.

THE REAL STEP ON THE PATH

We each approach the abyss in our own way. It may even be that this abyss appears without any context, just as a feeling, raw and intense. Betrayal or abandonment may throw us into an instinctual anguish so primal and powerful that the very root of our existence seems to be being attacked, assaulted by an unknown force. And this abyss is so terrible that we will try to turn away, even hide ourself in the arms of a tangible lover.

But this abyss is always waiting. It is the doorway to the infinite, the emptiness through which all travelers must pass. Beyond the doorway the terror subsides as the single ray of His love absorbs us. The abyss is His drawing us to Him, drawing us into the circle of His love for us, a love so total that we are no longer present. The abyss carries the power of His presence, which for the ego is desolation, for the mind is bewilderment, but for the soul is the only way Home. Yet until we arrive at this abyss we cannot even imagine it or be prepared for the feelings that it evokes.

We search for Him, we climb the long arduous path up the mountain. What we find is never what we expect. We expected to arrive, and instead find a black hole that draws us, a vortex of power that pulls us, and our most primal fear holds us back. Rûmî tells the story of a man who went in search of a lion:

> The rumor of a great lion spread throughout the world. A man wanted to see the lion and for a year endured all the hardships of the journey and travelled from place to place. When he arrived at the forest and saw the lion from a distance, he came to a sudden halt. He couldn't move and couldn't go any further.

Someone who knew the lion said to the man gently, "You've come such a long way out of love for the lion. Know this about him: if you go toward him bravely and tenderly stoke him, he will not harm you in any way; if you are afraid, he will be furious. Sometimes he even attacks people who are scared of him, howling, 'How dare you have such a black opinion of me!' You've endured a year of bitter difficulty to get here to see him. Why are you standing still now that you are so close? Take one more step toward him!"

No one could find in themselves the courage to advance even one step. Everyone said, "Every step we took before this was easy. Here, we cannot move."

It takes immense faith to come towards the Lion in the presence of the Lion. That step is a majestic and noble act, one that only the Elect and Friends of God are capable of. This is the real step on the Path; all the other steps are just vanishing footprints. And the faith required to take it comes only to saints and prophets, to those who have washed their hands of their own life.[15]

The lion is the path which pulls us to Him. A spiritual path is a dynamic energy that comes from the beyond and prepares us for the sacrifice of our own self. The path draws us to Him with the call of love, with the heart's desire for what is Real. But suddenly, one day, we find ourself in the presence of the path, at the entrance to the arena of love, an arena whose floor is bloody with slain victims. We suddenly know the lion will devour us, know it not with our mind, not with any preconceived idea of spiritual surrender, but in our guts, with our whole instinctual self holding back in horror.

We feel what it means to be love's victim, not as some spiritual ideal, but as a wind that howls through us, terrifying every fiber. "To die before death" suddenly becomes an agony of indecision. Do we dare to go forward? Are we crazy enough? What about all the values we brought with us, all of our beliefs and spiritual ideas? That which is most precious has to go—for myself it was the knowledge that I belonged to Him. So He sold me into the slavery of a world without Him, and it took me a lifetime to accept it.

To say yes to abandonment is a suicide pact with our Beloved, a dance of death in which we give ourself entirely. And His lovers die with a smile on their lips, the smile of longing being lived to its fullest. When al-Hallâj was on the cross and had his hands and feet cut off he was asked, "What is Sufism?" He replied, "Its lowest degree you are seeing now." "And its highest degree?" Al-Hallâj replied, "...Tomorrow you will see ... for I witness it in divine mystery."[16] And the next day his head was cut off. In his crucifixion al-Hallâj enacted love's mystery on the world's outer stage. But the same inner commitment is demanded of all lovers who dare to give themselves in love, who knowingly take the "real step" towards the lion while in the presence of the lion. And, as Rûmî simply states, "the faith required to take it comes only to saints and prophets, to those who have washed their hands of their own life."

The lion, the path, is the abyss. This abyss *is* the emptiness which is the fullness of love. Stepping into the abyss, taking that step towards the lion, is a giving of ourself to love. But this love is so different from anything we could conceive that it appears as a terrible, bottomless chasm, as a devouring primal power. Only lovers who carry an imprint, a memory of the taste of real love, of the "wine drunk before the creation of the vine," are called by this memory over the edge, into the craziness of an inborn intoxication, the soul's addiction to what is limitless and real.

And what happens beyond the abyss? Nothing "happens" because the lover is dead. This is the conundrum that Rûmî tries to express:

> A grammar lesson: "The lover died."
>   "Lover" is subject and agent, but that can't be!
>   The "lover" is defunct.

> Only grammatically is the dervish-lover a doer.

> In reality, with he or she so overcome,
>   so dissolved into love,
>   all qualities of doing-ness
>   disappear.[17]

What is it that dies? What is this dissolution? To the one who stands in front of the lion, at the edge of the abyss, it seems so final, so ultimate. But the lion is ourself, our real inner nature. The abyss is the emptiness that is at the core of our being. The abyss is the freedom of what we really are, not the illusion in which we imprison ourself. The lion is the love that is "what we were before we were." Losing ourself is like shedding an old winter coat and finally feeling the sunshine. This sunshine is the substance of love that has no limits, barriers, or beliefs. The reason the abyss can feel so cold is that it does not warm the personality; it does not embrace the ego. The "I" is left in its mortuary of isolation.

The "I" remains at the edge, feeling excluded, feeling the desolation of non-being, without being immersed in the bliss of real freedom, the intoxication of real love. Later the ego will be given a taste of the soul's joy; a reflection of the sunshine will permeate even this mirage, this semblance of self. The wayfarer, the lover, will feel the wonder of surrender, of knowing that he or she has been given to. What has been given we cannot know, because it is beyond the small horizon of our sense of self. But we can see the sunrise reflected on the distant mountains. We know that something has happened, that in the circle of love something has been given and received.

Oneness is not a mathematical equation but a living presence infused into our very being. The lion lives this presence, is this presence alive within us. When we are ready, when we are prepared for desolation, the lion appears. We may have thought that we were seeking the lion, but we were always the prey. The abyss is our longing that calls to us, dragging us to the edge of ourself. Abandonment is terror, vulnerability, violation, and bliss. Abandonment has no pretenses or preoccupations. She is love without limits where life and death belong together.

When we come to this edge, those who have gone before us may encourage us, speak of what we would long for, tell true lovers' tales. But finally, the choice is for each of us. We are not allowed to know what awaits us. We have to give a blank check of all our self, surrender in terror without expectation. Alone we stand at the edge of His aloneness. Maybe, one day, we will dare to jump.

FORGETFULNESS

Forgetfulness is a divine attribute.

Ibn 'Arabî[1]

THE MYSTERY OF FORGETTING

Recently I was sitting in an airport lounge full of people waiting to board a flight. For a few moments my eyes were opened, and I saw how each person was full of His presence, how there was nothing other than He, His light, His love, His beauty. And in the same few moments I also saw that these people did not know it. In this experience I realized that the real mystery is not that we are all divine, are filled with His substance, but that we do not know it. *We do not know that we are a part of God.* This experience filled me with wonder, the wonder that part of the mystery of creation is that we have been allowed to forget Him. It is His will that in us He forgets Himself, just as it is His will that He allows us to remember Him.

Many souls live their whole life in forgetfulness, never consciously knowing their own divine nature. But some souls are awakened into remembrance, and become wayfarers searching for Him. Yet even those whose hearts have been awakened, who have been implanted with the seed of divine remembrance, turn away from the path and forget Him. Not every wayfarer finds his way Home, comes to know consciously the nature of his divinity. So many seekers are distracted and lose the thread of their remembrance.

Why do seekers leave the path? Why do wayfarers turn away from their quest, lovers hide themselves from their Beloved? Is the ego so strong that it can divert the will of God? Are His veils so impenetrable that He is hidden entirely? If the whole world is God, why has He forgotten Himself, and why does He allow even His servants, even those who seek Him out, to turn away from Him?

Is the road too difficult, the path too long and steep? Are the distractions too many? So many seekers begin with enthusiasm and then stumble, are diverted, sidetracked back into the world. Yet spiritual life is so simple, so clear. The heart looks towards God and God looks towards the heart. The essential truth of "He loves them and they love Him" is stamped into the core of creation. So why is it so easily avoided?

Is it because we have to face ourself, our dark side, our fears and insecurities, because we have to become vulnerable and unsure? Or is the pain awakened by His presence too intolerable? Why does He tempt us with such a promise, a dream of tremendous bliss, and then leave us to wander away, to be distracted?

The duel between the ego and the Self is so one-sided. The Self is so strong, eternal, all-powerful. So why does the ego win so many times? Is it because the Self cannot use its power, is forbidden to reveal its real nature?

Why do we not want to know what we really are? Why are we content with so little? Even when He has given us a glimpse of what is real, why do we run away, hide ourself from the simple splendor of our true nature? Why is the path so precarious when He is the foundation, the substance of everything? Why would anyone want to forget Him, not desire to remember this eternal love affair? We are lost without Him, and yet we live in this lostness, exist from day to day, work and make love, have children and have debts, all without acknowledging what is real.

Is He really so cruel, so much of a trickster? He tempts us with His presence. He opens the gates of remembrance, and then veils the entrance. He veils it with our own illusory self, with our "I," with what we think we are, and then watches us stumble around in this darkness of our forgetfulness. He helps us to remember and then allows us to forget.

Everything is His will. Our remembrance is His will and our forgetting is His will. In the closed circle of love, in the oneness of His real nature, nothing is lost, nothing is found. And yet again and again we lose ourself, and sometimes, with His grace, we are allowed to find ourself, to uncover what was always there. And again and again we are diverted from the quest, from the work of uncovering. Sometimes a particular veil is so beautiful we do not want to remove it, but become enthralled by its tapestry, by the colors woven into its texture. Or a veil is engrossing in its darkness, in the problems and distortions it presents. Sometimes our complexities, our doubts, and our weaknesses are more captivating than the simple light of His love.

Why He does this to Himself we can never know, because He is so far beyond us, "beyond even our idea of the beyond." But many sincere seekers who begin with enthusiasm and diligence, who are allowed to remember for a moment and then follow this remembrance, are diverted from their quest. Only too soon they forget; they follow a path that leads back to the ego, back to the pettiness and limited horizon of the little self. In our forgetfulness He forgets Himself, just as in our remembrance He remembers Himself. What part do we have to play in this eternal drama? What is the responsibility of the seeker, the duty of the lover? Are we just thrown hither and thither in the sea of unknowing, or can we bring into consciousness the soul's desire to go Home, the lover's longing for her Beloved, and live this longing until there are no distractions, until He is our whole focus?

THE ONE QUALITY NEEDED

Remembrance is at the core of the path. Before the soul came into the world it pledged to remember Him, to witness that He is Lord. This is our Primordial Covenant and the work of the wayfarer is to honor this covenant. This work of remembrance is the substance of the journey. Remembrance is an awakening to our deepest purpose, the work of witnessing Him in His world. In the words of Rûmî it is the "one thing in the world which you must never forget."

> There is one thing in the world which you must never forget. If you were to forget everything else and remembered this, then you would have nothing at all to worry about; but if you were to remember everything else and then forget this, you would have done nothing with your life.
>
> It is as if a king sent you to a country to carry out a particular mission. You go to that country, you do a hundred different things; but if you do not perform the mission assigned to you, it is as if you have done nothing. All human beings come into the world for a particular mission,

and that mission is our singular purpose. If we do not enact it, we have done nothing....

Now if you were to say, "Look, even if I have not performed this mission I have, after all, performed a hundred others," that would mean nothing. You were not created for those other missions. It is as if you were to buy a sword of priceless Indian steel such as one usually finds only in the treasures of emperors, and were to turn it into a butcher's knife for cutting up rotten meat, saying, "Look, I'm not letting this sword stay unused, I am putting it to a thousand highly useful purposes." Or it is as though you were to take a golden bowl and cook turnips in it, while for just one grain of that gold you could purchase hundreds of pots.

Or it is as though you were to take a dagger of the most finely-wrought and tempered steel and use it as a nail to hang a broken pitcher on, saying, "I'm making excellent use of my dagger. I'm hanging a broken pitcher on it, after all." When you could hang a picture on a nail that costs only a few cents, what sense does it make to use a dagger worth a fortune?

> You are more valuable than both heaven
>   and earth.
> What else can I say? You don't know
>   your own worth.
> Do not sell yourself at a ridiculous price,
> You who are so valuable in God's eyes.[2]

He is the substance of our being and yet is hidden from us. He is so near to us, and so far away; and we need Him and we forget Him. The very fact that we look for Him, that we begin the search, means that He has implanted within us the need to remember Him. He turns our heart towards Him, infuses us with the light of remembrance, and so we begin the search. This is the blissful beginning of the journey.

The difficulty is that this bliss, this light of remembrance, does not belong to the level of the ego, but belongs to the soul. The soul remembers God, and the ego and our lower nature veil us from this remembrance. In the experience of *tauba* (the turning of the heart), the power of His love pierces through the veils of the ego. For a moment we are lifted into the dimension of the soul, where His love for us and our love for Him shine so clearly. In this instant we remember; the lover remembers her Beloved. Then we return to the ego; the light fades, and we are left with a remembrance of our remembrance. The work then is to live this remembrance, before it "fades into the light of common day."

The awakening of our remembrance is so sweet because it belongs to the soul. It gives us a taste of our eternal nature, of the honey that was before the bee. But because it belongs to the soul it is so difficult to hold when we are back in the ego. Remembrance of God does not belong to the ego or the mind. The ego does not understand what is pre-eternal; the mind cannot grasp a dimension of light upon light. So we are left stranded, bombarded by doubts. Is it real? Is it worthwhile? Am I allowed to live this dream? Later, much later, when the mind and ego have become permeated by the light of His presence, such questions will fall away, be dissolved. But at the beginning they are powerful, and easily distort the inner experience we are given. They carry the density of this world and the contradictions of our lower nature. They seem so substantial compared with the intangible touch of His love.

The mind, the ego, the *nafs* make us forget; we forget our mission of remembrance, our singular purpose. We do not value what we have been given; we do not recognize its true worth. The lover is lost, stranded on the further shores of love, and thus returns to the familiar patterns of the mind and the desires of the ego. Can we remember without the power of His presence? His grace will carry us to Him, but are we open to His grace? The mind and the ego close the doors, separating us from the experience we have been given. The power of forgetfulness is to entice us to remain with what we know, with what is only too familiar. The prison walls of our conditioning are comforting and reassuring.

THE PLACE OF FORGETFULNESS

Again and again He allows us to forget. We are busy; we do many things except the one thing that matters. Our need to remember Him becomes buried in daily life, in outer activities, in all the preoccupations with which we cover ourself. But how can we forget that which is more precious than life, that we belong to Him and have pledged to witness Him? How can we dismiss this primal purpose, allow ourself to slip back into unconsciousness when so much has been done to awaken us?

We are confronted by all the difficulties of the path, the struggle with the *nafs*, and the need to control the mind. These are our problems, which we need to fight or accept according to our own nature, according to our attributes. But forgetfulness haunts us, surrounds us on every side, waylays us, seduces us, until the path peters out, and we do not even notice it. And He allows us to forget Him, to be waylaid. He is like a lover who allows his beloved to be seduced by another, and just watches, without interfering. He allows us to lose that which is most precious—our knowledge of His love.

At the Primordial Covenant our soul pledged itself to witness Him. But when we are born into this world we are carried into forgetfulness. Ibn 'Arabî describes this "fall" into "the place of forgetfulness":

> Original faith is the primordial nature in accordance with which God created mankind. It is their witnessing to His Oneness at the taking of the Covenant. Hence every child is born in keeping with that Covenant. However, when he falls by means of the body into the confines of Nature—the place of forgetfulness—he becomes ignorant and forgets the state which he had had with his Lord.[3]

In the eyes of a child remembrance still shines; the veils between the two worlds have not yet fully fallen into place. A story is told of a three-year-old boy who has just been presented with a baby sister. The three-year-old insists to his parents that he wants to be alone with his sister. Knowing the dangers of sibling rivalry the parents are apprehensive, but the boy insists so much that they finally give in. However, they take the precaution of listening to the "child minder" that is in the baby's room. What they hear is the boy approaching his sister and asking with great urgency, "You must tell me about God. I'm beginning to forget."

This same story is told a different way in a dream a friend had about her young child. In the dream the father is saying, "Shouldn't he be learning to talk?" But as the mother listens to the father's concerns, she hears her child singing, "And we remember Him." The child that has not yet learned to talk is singing the remembrance of God.

Growing up in a world of forgetfulness, the child forgets, and, in the words of e.e. cummings, "down they forgot as up they grew."[4] When I heard this dream of the boy singing His remembrance I wondered if the child forgets because he is surrounded by forgetfulness; there is no echo to his remembrance. Could it be that if the mother remembers, the child does not have to forget? If she sings the remembrance of God in her heart, upon her lips, her child will be able to avoid the desert of forgetfulness? Or do we need to forget? Is forgetfulness a part of our journey? Coming into creation, the soul takes the clothes of manifestation, the human form. The human form is made in the image of God, but, according to Ibn 'Arabî, because of this form "man possessed the potentiality to forget his servanthood." Angels do not forget, but human beings, made in His image, forget. "God described man by forgetfulness (*nisyân*) since He said concerning Adam, 'He forgot' (Qur'an 20:115)." But Ibn 'Arabî continues by saying,

> Forgetfulness is a divine attribute.... Hence [by forgetting] we do not deviate from what we are. God said, "They forgot God, so He forgot them" (Qur'an 9:67) in the manner that is appropriate to His majesty.[5]

He gives us the experience of His forgetfulness. Coming into the world of forms which is also the instinctual world of the Great Mother, we embrace forgetfulness. Her forms capture us with fascination and desires; instincts carry us into unconsciousness, draw us into the unending cycle of life and death. Forgetfulness is the poison of the Great Mother as she makes us believe we exist only here, in her physical, instinctual world, in the multitude of her forms. In her world there is no remembrance, just desires, the drives that carry us through life: food, shelter, sex. The Great Mother is the world of forgetfulness in which only our instincts need to be satisfied.

We experience forgetfulness only too easily, but once we are awakened to remember, how can we counter the pull into unconsciousness of the Great Mother, the distraction of her many forms? Ascetics fight her, turning away from her forms, denying their instinctual needs. They use the sword of conscious will to do battle with her feminine power. The danger is that this gives even more power to the instincts, because repressed, they carry the energy of the shadow. The ascetic becomes polarized, denying his own nature, rejecting the feminine. He is haunted by the demons of his repressed self, and also denies himself the passionate nature of the quest, the instinctual hunger of the soul's desire to remember God. So much potential then becomes locked in the unconscious, in the arena of forgetfulness.

Could it be that although the Great Mother carries us into forgetfulness, she also holds a secret of remembrance, the secret that is hidden in the word of creation, "*Kun!*" [Be]? Our Beloved sent us into His world in order to remember Him; this is "our particular mission." Why should we deny His world in order to remember Him? How many times has a sunrise reminded me, a flight of wild birds stirred something within me, the eyes of a child haunted me? Even images of dejection have turned me to Him; a homeless man with his few belongings mirrored my own emptiness.

Within His world we experience His forgetfulness and are then awakened to His remembrance. In the moment of awakening we recognize the desolation of our forgetfulness—the emptiness of a world in which we do not see His face. The work is then to stick to the primal purpose that comes into consciousness with our awakening—the soul's covenant to witness His oneness.

"Lead us not into temptation," says the Lord's Prayer. How His world tempts us, attracts us, deceives us![6] But once the wayfarer is awakened he carries a quality of consciousness that reveals what is hidden within creation: the one face within the many. In the words of Jâmî,

> Since they have turned towards God in complete spiritual nudity by wholly emptying their hearts of all worldly attachments ... and persevering along this path without slackening, interruption of thought or dissolution of will, God has granted them a revealing light to show them things as they really are. This light appears within at the appearance of a level beyond the level of the intellect.[7]

With this light the wayfarer can see beneath the world of appearances. When we turn towards Him and begin the long journey Home, life can become a mirror of revelation, and within our instinctual self we find the primal power of our need to witness Him. The place of forgetfulness becomes a workshop of remembrance.

THE HIDDEN POWER OF LOVE

Love is the secret catalyst of remembrance. If we love someone, we think of him, we remember him. How much more powerful is our love for Him who is love! This is the mystery of "light upon light": as the light of our consciousness turns towards Him, His light comes to meet us and helps to reveal what is hidden. The people of love who have turned away from the world and turned back to Him are granted this light.

With the light of His love we can see the secret face of creation. We can experience His presence which is within all of existence; we can see beneath the surface to where His name is engraved upon every atom. In the oneness of love we can see His oneness, the oneness that permeates all of His world:

> Invoke the One—desire the One—search the
>   One
>   See the One—know the One and affirm that
>   it is One
> Whether at the beginning or at the end, all of
>   this is only one single thing
>   ... Because each atom has a secret tie with
>   Him
> See the name and see the significance, "All is
>   You."[8]

Our love for Him and His love for us form a circle of remembrance in which we come to know the oneness that is inside and outside. When we live this love we bring His mystery into the plane of manifestation, the mystery of oneness and multiplicity, the mystery of a world that appears to have forgotten Him. With the eye of the heart we see how every atom sings His praises, how nothing has ever forgotten Him. We consciously experience the wonder of His eternal remembrance. The illusion of His forgetfulness is lifted aside, as we recognize what our innermost heart has always known, that we play a part in His consciousness of His eternal Self, in His remembrance of Himself.

Yet in the circle of love's oneness there is neither forgetting nor remembrance, because forgetting and remembrance belong to duality and to the illusion of separation. In love's eternal moment there is only the now of knowing, knowing that we cannot know Him, just as we cannot forget Him. The work of the wayfarer is to live this eternal moment—the witnessing of the heart—while existing also in the dimension of duality, amidst the multiplicity of His world. Then the creation is no longer a distraction, but an expression of His majesty and His beauty, a place to wonder and worship Him:

> Since it is not possible for you to have access
>   to His Essence
> Console yourself in contemplating the beauty
>   of creation![9]

One of the paradoxes of the path is that we carry love's hidden secret and yet have forgotten it. We work to remember what we have always known. We have to walk this road, struggling to focus on the singular purpose of remembering Him. Again and again we are distracted, again and again we bring our attention back to Him whom our heart loves. We try to stay faithful to this first love, and through the practices of the path, meditation, *dhikr*, watchfulness, we keep our focus.

Many times we are distracted and tested by distractions. Many times our instincts overwhelm us and carry us into forgetfulness, until we are rescued by the deeper instinct of our need for Him. Each time we reawaken to our forgetfulness we feel remorse, yet we should not blame ourself, because that is just ego. Rather we should thank Him for reminding us, and continue with the slow, arduous work of changing a consciousness that is caught in the ego to a consciousness that is held by His presence. We aspire to arrive at a place where we can no longer forget Him, where remembrance permeates so much of us that the heart rules over the ego. The wayfarer who has arrived at this station has become His witness:

> The people of witnessing and finding surpass others. Though the attribute may be the same, he who knows his station with God is not like him who does not know it. "Say: 'Are they equal—those who know and those who know not?' Only those who possess the kernels remember" (Qur'an 39:9). This verse tells us that they knew, then forgetfulness overcame some of them. Some of them continue to be ruled by the property of forgetfulness. "They forgot God, so He forgot them" (Qur'an 9:67). Others are reminded and remember. These are the "possessors of the kernels."[10]

"The Folk of Allâh are the people of the kernels. The kernel is their food."[11] The people of Allâh are nourished by their remembrance and by His companionship, for He has promised "I am the companion of him who remembers Me."[12] Only He gives them sustenance, while those who have forgotten have to be nourished by themselves—"They forgot God so God forgot them."

WE BELONG TO HIM, AND HE DOES WITH US WHAT HE WISHES

This world throws us into the abyss of forgetfulness, in which it appears that we are forgotten by God. In this abyss we are tested: those who remember are remembered, while those who forget are forgotten. Al-Hakîm at-Tirmidhî tells a story of this test of forgetfulness in which the destinies of men were decreed:

> Abû 'Abdallâh [al-Hakîm at-Tirmidhî] said: On the day in which the destinies [of men] were decreed (*yawn al-maqâdîr*) God created them and they shone like brilliant stars. Then He withdrew the light from them and He placed them within the earthliness of the soil-element from which He designed the creation of Adam, peace be upon him.... In this darkness deprived of light, they abided some fifty thousand years or so. And during this period of time in which they were in darkness they became three groups. One group said: "He who ruled over us does not rule any more; His kingship has ceased and He lost His power over it. If this were not so, He would not have left us here forgotten." The second group said: "He left us here, and we shall wait and see what will be and what will befall us from Him." The first group were non-believers and the second group displayed duplicity and doubt. And the third group said: "He left us here and He is eternal. We belong to Him, and He does with us what He wishes."

As for the first group, when they spoke the way they did, the soil filled their mouths and He said to them: "What have you seen from Me that you ascribed to Me impotence and the loss of kingship?" Hence, this word [= the word of Godfearing: *lâ ilâha illâ 'llâh*] became a seal of soil on their mouths ... and the seal is never removed.

The second group displayed doubt; in their disbelief they waited to see how things would turn up, having no certitude, their hearts wavering. Hence, the soil-element was strewn about the mouths of their hearts to make them vacillate: at times turning toward God and at times turning away from Him and at times turning toward the *nafs*. It did not become a seal but a padlock, which—if He wishes—can be removed and opened. But the seal is never removed....

As for the third group, they said: "Our Lord who rules over us is eternal, and He does with us what He wishes: If He wishes He places us in darkness, and if He wishes He places us in light." Then they stretched out the hands of their hearts toward Him to attach themselves to Him. And He struck their hearts with His hands and said: "You are mine, whether you practice or whether you don't practice." Hence this word became written upon their hearts. Those who were struck by His right hand, they are the Friends (*al-awliyâ'*), and those who were struck by His other hand are the ordinary [monotheistic] believers (*al-muwahhidûn*). He took hold of them and placed them within His

> grip, and this word became written on their
> inner hearts (*qulûb*) in front of the eyes of the
> outer heart (*fu'âf*). Hence He said: "He
> wrote the faith (*îmân*) upon their hearts...."[13]

In this remarkable passage at-Tirmidhî describes
three different responses to the soul's descent from a
world of light into the darkness of this world. Here in
this world where His light and love are no longer so
visible, it appears that He has forgotten us. In this state
of apparent abandonment we are tested. Do we forget
Him, do we doubt Him, or do we remember Him and
acknowledge that we belong to Him regardless of
where He places us?

Those who reject Him because it appears that they
are rejected have their mouths sealed with the soil of this
world. They will remain in the state of forgetfulness
which they have chosen for themselves. "They forgot
God so God forgot them." The second group whose
hearts waver due to their doubts are without certitude.
Their hearts turn sometimes towards God and sometimes
towards their lower self, the *nafs*. Sometimes they remember but then they forget. If He wishes He can open
the padlock and bring them into a state of perpetual
remembrance.

Finally the third group are those who acknowledge
that they belong to Him even when He appears to
abandon them. Their remembrance does not depend
upon their circumstance. "We belong to Him, and He
does with us what He wishes." In this arena the wayfarer
is tested and tested, but he acknowledges His Lord
irrespective of what happens to him—"If He wishes He
places us in darkness, and if He wishes He places us in
light." This degree of surrender and remembrance is
demanded of those who are destined to belong to Him:

"And He struck their hearts with His hands and said: 'You are mine, whether you practice or whether you don't practice.'"

In the darkness of this world we are tested by His forgetfulness. Do we forget Him because He appears to have forgotten us, or can this place of abandonment be an opportunity to show our Beloved that we belong to Him whatever He wills? Our remembrance of Him should not depend upon our state, internal or external. Living our devotion without reference to our state, we pass through the veils of appearance, pass beyond His apparent forgetfulness. We pass into the oneness of the real relationship of the soul and God, in which there is neither remembrance nor forgetfulness. Both remembrance and forgetfulness belong to duality: in the oneness of true love, who is there to remember and who is there to forget? In the closed circle of His love we belong to Him beyond duality.

The soul has pledged to witness Him and this pledge is written within the heart, written in the same words that state "You are mine." Those who belong to Him are here to witness Him: this is our pledge of belonging. We surrender to the world of separation for His sake, while within the heart we retain knowledge of His oneness. Living in the world, we experience His multiplicity and offer it back to Him; thus we come to know the wonder of oneness within multiplicity.

How can He ever forget Himself? This is a part of the illusion of this world, and those who have passed beyond this illusion know Him in a way that cannot be forgotten. It may appear that we forget Him, but how can a lover ever forget her Beloved? Then she is no longer a lover.

Falling into this world, we experience His apparent forgetfulness, because He needs us to experience it:

He needs us to know this aspect of Himself. But we only know that we have forgotten Him when we are awakened to remember Him. Those whose forgetfulness remains, who are sealed with the soil of this world, *do not know that they have forgotten Him.* Knowledge of forgetfulness is the first step in our remembrance.

When I met my teacher I came to know for how long I had forgotten. Over the years the desolation of this forgetfulness haunted me, the horror that I had to live without recognizing Him or knowing that I belonged to Him. Life without the knowledge of His presence, or the purpose to witness Him, was a state of abandonment too terrible to fully accept. I had lived it, but when I came to know it I resented it. I resented the fact that I had been so abandoned. Maybe through His grace I can come to recognize that I needed to forget Him, that I needed to experience the emptiness of a world without Him—how His world appears when His face is not seen reflected.

Once we experience how His presence permeates everything, the wonder is that we do not always know it. This was my experience in the airport lounge, as I was surrounded by people who did not know that they are a part of God. How can we not see of what we are made, feel the sunshine that gives warmth and light to everything? How can we forget our own deepest self? But just as we can never come to know our Beloved, so are the mysteries of creation beyond our understanding. Yet slowly the veils of duality that cover us can be stripped away, until everything, even His forgetfulness, His abandonment, is seen as stamped with His name. In the words of al-Hallâj, "As far as I am concerned, if I am forsaken it is Your abandonment that keeps me company."[14]

THE INVISIBLE CENTER

A time will come when the tongue will join the heart,
the heart will join the soul,
the soul will join the secret (sirr)
and the secret will join the Truth (Haqq).
The heart will say to the tongue, "Keep silent!"
The secret will say to the soul, "Keep silent!"
And the inward light will say to the secret,
"Keep silent!"

Al-Ansârî[1]

THE CIRCLE OF WHOLENESS

Stepping onto the path we step into the circle of our own wholeness. During the first few years on the path a wonderful healing takes places as the different and contradictory aspects of our self come together, contained by the circle of our wholeness. We are allowed to be ourself in the deepest and most complete way. The profound nature of this acceptance cannot be exaggerated *because it is complete.* In the circle of the Self *nothing is excluded*; everything is recognized as a part of the whole, a necessary note in the symphony of our true being.

When I first arrived at my teacher's door I felt this acceptance, and for the first time in my life I knew that I was recognized and allowed to be. The nature of this acceptance was so primal that the mind did not register it until later; the knowing came as a feeling of coming home, a relaxation so deep that there was no comparison. For weeks, for months, I just sat in deep amazement at the unconscious awareness that there were no inner boundaries, no constrictions, no holding back. The knowledge that *I was accepted for myself,* without conditions, was so revolutionary and yet so necessary. Years later I was able to pass on this simple truth to a woman who came to our group, saying to her, "Don't try to fit in. Here you are allowed to be yourself."

So much in our life we constrict and limit ourself, push ourself into corners and cut ourself into socially acceptable pieces. A Sufi group is based upon oneness, and the essential quality of this oneness is that everything is a part of His sacred wholeness—there is nothing other than He. This is illustrated in the story of the great Sufi, Jâmî, who, when walking in the streets after curfew time, intoxicated with God, was apprehended by the officer of the watch. The officer naively asked him if he was a thief, and Jâmî replied, "What am I not?"

Coming to the path, we enter this sacred wholeness in which His oneness is honored and lived. Sufis are the "people of the secret" because they know and live His secret, the oneness of lover and Beloved, a oneness that includes all of creation and yet does not deny His transcendent nature. There is a quality of consciousness that sees the oneness in all life, and recognizes it as a reflection of His Oneness. In the mirror of creation we glimpse the beauty of His Face: "Wheresoever you turn, there is the Face of Allâh." And yet within the heart we know that this is just a reflection of His unknowable, unreachable Essence.

The oneness at the core of the path slowly heals the wayfarer, making him whole. This is a miracle to watch, as wayfarers who have been wounded by life, cut off from their true self, are slowly redeemed. I experienced this happening within myself, how a broken human being hovering on the border of a nervous breakdown was brought back to life. I arrived as a wounded bird and my wings were healed, and I was able to live the honesty and simple wonder of being human. Over the years I have seen it happen to others, how they are given back their dignity and slowly sense the integrity of their innate nature. Then life is no longer lived as a discord, as a series of conflicts, but in harmony with something greater.

How this process happens carries the inexplicable quality of every miracle. It is given as a gift, for, like the sunshine, our true Self is free and is our birthright. I remember clearly when I had the simple realization, "I am allowed to be myself, and to live myself." And with this there came the understanding that there is a place in the world for each of us as our true self. We do not have to cut ourself into pieces in order to fit into the world. He made us each according to His will: we are made in the image of God and carry a unique imprint of His nature. And because it is His world, there must be a place for each of us where we can live our real self. This revelation awoke such a joy within me that I knew it belonged to life itself. And it brought with it a freedom and sense of expansion that made me buoyant for days.

DESCENT INTO DARKNESS

There is, of course, a price to be paid for this journey into wholeness. One of the paradoxes of the path is that although spiritual things are given, as a gift, we have to pay with our own blood and tears to be able to receive them. We have to be torn apart in order to be made whole. The first years on the path bring discord as well as healing. We are taken on a descent into the darkness of the unconscious, into the wounds of our own shadowlands. Irina Tweedie describes the intensity of her own experience with her teacher, and how it was not what she expected:

> I hoped to get instuctions in Yoga, expected wonderful teachings, but what the Teacher did was mainly to force me to face the darkness within myself, and it almost killed me.[2]

Traditionally the darkness is the place of our rebirth. In the unconscious we find all the unaccepted aspects of our own psyche that need to be integrated if we are to live our rediscovered wholeness. Psychologically this usually begins with a confrontation with our shadow, the dark, denied part of ourself, full of unpleasant and unacknowledged feelings as well as unlived potential.[3] Confrontation with the shadow is a warrior's work that demands patience, perseverance, and integrity, as we are forced to accept that we are not the person we think we are, but carry within us a darker twin. Anger, cruelty, bitterness, greed, and a host of other despised qualities come to the surface, needing love and acceptance. We also come to feel the pain of the rejected parts of ourself, the wounds which they carry.

Our wholeness is given back to us by the path, but we have to work to integrate it. We have to find the strength to bring our darkness into the light and suffer its unlived anguish, and in this process experience our ego being broken and remade by the powerful forces of the unconscious. The opposites within us attack each other, seeking dominance, and we suffer the pain of no longer living on the surface of our life.

Only by accepting our faults and failings can we master them, as the power of the shadow is then con-tained by consciousness and love. The potency of our shadow is that it dominates us without our knowing, as we suddenly explode into destructive anger or retreat into passive aggression. Jung wisely remarked, "You do not have a shadow but the shadow has you."

As shadow work reconnects us to rejected parts of our own self, we experience an increase in energy and potential. Feelings locked in the depths are allowed into our life, bringing with them a deeper and more complete sense of our own nature, and a liberation of the energy we had been using to keep these qualities locked up in our inner basement or dungeon. In our dreams we relate to inner figures who before had appeared as threatening; we share meals, may even become lovers. Often this inner work is imaged as clearing out rubbish, freeing ourself from the inner debris we have accumulated during our life, even inherited from our parents and grandparents. The more inner space we have, the more our life can expand, both inwardly and outwardly. Gradually we allow ourself more space and discover unlived potential. As our sense of self expands, in our dreams we discover that the house of our psyche has more rooms, even whole floors that we never knew existed, waiting to be inhabited.

Accepting our darkness gives our ego a balance and integrity that are often lacking in someone who knows only his conscious identity. As the light becomes balanced by the dark, the fragmented sense of our self begins to change into a deep sense of well-being and wholeness. We cease being isolated within the castle of our consciousness, fearful of our inner demons. We are no longer haunted survivors or troubled victims of our childhood traumas. And we begin to see life from the perspective of one who has visited the underworld— prejudices and judgments fall away when we come to know the dark side of our own nature. No longer bounded by the limited horizon of ego consciousness, we open to life's infinite possibilities. The fullness of life begins to reveal itself as we honor the contradictory qualities that create our own completeness.

The path constellates our wholeness and gives us a taste of our true nature. The years of laborious and painful inner work allow us to live this wholeness. Many of the wounds with which we arrived on the path are healed as a deep transformation takes place. We are healed both by our own work and by the grace that is given. It is a wonder to experience this redemption, to look back and realize with awe and gratitude that so many wounds have been healed, painful problems dissolved. This change is often so deep and fundamental that there is little trace left of the traumas that dominated our life, and we can almost forget the person we were. Recently I tried to recreate the feelings I had when I first came to the path, and realized how difficult it is to remember a time before love was present, to remember the fragmented, isolated sense of my own self that dominated my every day. I only know that I have been changed beyond recognition and given an experience of life that I did not believe possible. I have tasted the true joy of being alive.

THE IMPRINT WITHIN THE HEART

There is a special grace given to those who seek Him. Looking towards Him, even in the darkness of our confusion and brokenness, we attract His light. This light is the power that heals us, that remakes us according to His imprint that we carry within us. This imprint is stamped within the heart, and is activated by the energy of the path, the power of love. The more we look towards Him, the more we open to our Beloved, the more this imprint is ignited with the light of His love. The eleventh-century Sufi, Ansârî of Herât, describes how this imprint of our heart's friendship with Him becomes the lamp of our divine consciousness:

> The way to find friendship
>> is to toss this world and the Hereafter
>>> into the sea.
> The sign of the realization of friendship
>> is to not take care of anything that is not
>>> God.
> The beginning of friendship is to have an
> imprint;
>> the end is having a lamp.[4]

Our friendship with Him whom we love is a secret hidden within the heart. This secret is the hidden face of the mystic, one who belongs to God since before she was born. The work of the path is to clean and purify an inner space within which the secret, *sirr*, can be born into consciousness. We have to give birth to a quality of consciousness that can bear the brightness of His light, a consciousness pure enough to witness His love. According to the Sufis the *sirr* belongs to the innermost recesses of the heart, and it is here that the real mystical experiences take place, as the lover comes to know the nature of her friendship with her Beloved.

Yet this meeting place is so secret that the everyday consciousness of the wayfarer does not have access. The consciousness that witnesses His presence is the higher consciousness of the Self. The ego is excluded from the mystery of *light upon light* that takes place within our own heart. Thus, while the inner work with the unconscious expands our sense of self and deepens our awareness, the real mystical process often seems to exclude us, to leave us unaware of what is happening within our own heart. Sometimes, in moments of ecstasy and bewilderment, we tune into our higher consciousness and are allowed to glimpse the wonder of what is happening within us, but days can pass with only a feeling of emptiness, even a coldness, as the heart's real love affair happens elsewhere. Furthermore, the meeting of lover and Beloved is actually a process of absorption, as the innermost substance of the lover becomes dissolved in His infinite ocean. Through inner work we found ourself, discovered our true nature. Now we begin to lose our self.

HIS REMEMBRANCE OF HIMSELF

For many years we identified the path with our own struggles and inner work. This work brought results, the rewards of individuation and feeling our own wholeness. We were able to partly transform our shadow[5] and then make a relationship with our inner partner, the god or goddess whom we first projected onto another and then discovered within ourself.[6]

Our inner partner brought strength and creativity into our life and a loving embrace into our dreams. We also developed a sense of our center, and through prayer and meditation found peace and an inner communion founded upon devotion.

These qualities which we develop are important stepping stones. They take us along the path, towards the core of our being. But they do not prepare us for the realization that the real mystical relationship which happens within the heart does not take place between ourself and our Beloved; we are at best only an occasional onlooker, as the following dream poignantly images:

> I was walking along the trail I walk with my dog each morning. I was just past where it crosses the creek when I saw Mohammed coming towards me on the trail. I saw that Mohammed was occupied with a practice: as he walked along the trail saying the name of God, whenever there was a special sweetness in His remembrance he was to establish a honey-bee hive a few feet past that spot. I saw Him throw a jar of honey down on the trail and knew that this was to mark the spot for the hive; I knew His name had come with a special sweetness just before he came into my view. I also knew that this new one would be the sixth honey-bee hive he'd established in that area just past the creek, a sort of gentle bowl in the hillside.

In this dream the Prophet Mohammed images the dreamer's innermost self, the being within her heart that is eternally occupied with His remembrance. This secret substance within the heart always looks towards God and is in constant communion with Him. This is the core of the mystical path, for the Sufi says that it is not you or I who is the real traveler on the path, the real lover, but a substance within the heart of hearts.

On her morning walk the dreamer meets her secret self walking towards her. But Mohammed is not concerned with the dreamer; he is occupied with his practice, repeating His name. It is always a startling revelation to realize that the path is not about us, that we are in many ways incidental. One of the dangers of spiritual work is that we can become so identified with our work upon ourself, our struggles and our progress, that we forget that the real spiritual activity is His remembrance of Himself that takes place deep within the heart. In fact, at the beginning of the dream the dreamer was slightly irritated to be disturbed in her daily walk, until she realized the nature of the encounter.

She was a witness of His remembrance of Himself, and saw that whenever this remembrance has a certain sweetness, something is left behind to mark the spot. A hive of honey bees is established so that others can come to know and taste the sweetness of His remembrance. His lovers bring a memory of His sweetness into the world, the sweetness of remembrance. Everything else is secondary—what we think of as our spiritual practice, our path, merely takes us to the place where we can witness His work, where we can meet Mohammed walking along the path just past the creek.

FORGETTING OUR FAULTS

Gradually the focus of our journey shifts from the inner work of "polishing the mirror of the heart" to the simplicity of living a daily life with a heart that belongs to God. The initial years of polishing are necessary to realize the heart's true nature, to glimpse how it can reflect His light into the world. But slowly the impetus that drove us inward, and forced us to face our demons and open to love, dissolves. The anguish and intensity of our initial aspiration seem no longer present. We may have learned to live a reasonably balanced life, to be able to still the mind in meditation (at least occasionally!); the *dhikr* may have become the foundation of our daily practice. But more and more we remain with ourself and with His hidden secret.

The self no longer seems to change or develop. Although we may have integrated some of our shadow, we still find some of our neuroses and anxieties present. We still may have conflicts in our relationships, difficulties in our job. We have not become a "perfect spiritual person," but an ordinary human being, and this can be disappointing. Western spiritual conditioning suggests some image of spiritual perfection, and does not prepare us for our ordinary self. The Zen wisdom of "chop wood and carry water" is much more realistic, and gives us the freedom to live an everyday life.

Psychological work is never over—there is always the inner housekeeping, and our dreams and reactions can still help us, keeping us aware of our shadow and daily psychological shifts. But more and more we have to learn to live with our own inadequacies and problems. Too much attention to inner work can become counterproductive, can be too ego-oriented. This is a delicate balance, as on the other hand our shadow can easily convince us that it is not worth bothering about at all. But the wayfarer knows that the purpose of the journey is not to become perfect, because only He is perfect, but to become His servant. As long as our inadequacies do not interfere with our work as His servant, why should we try to change them?

This shift away from our self is illustrated in the stages of repentance in Sarraj's *Book of Flashes.*[7] The work on the shadow can be equated with the first stage of repentance, which Sahl, an early Sufi from Iraq, describes as "to never forget your fault."[8] Becoming conscious of our faults is similar to confronting our darkness, except that shadow work demands that we accept our darkness, rather than turning away from it towards the light. But the next stage of repentance, as defined by the great tenth-century Sufi al-Junayd, is "forgetting your fault,"[9] the heart being so occupied with the remembrance of God that there is no concern for repentance. Neither our self nor our faults have any significance. The lover turns away from everything except Him; Sarraj quotes an-Nûrî, who, asked about repentance, said, "It is turning away from everything except God Most High."[10]

At the beginning of the path the wayfarer must focus on her own faults, which provides her with the self-understanding, strength, firmness, and purity necessary for the journey. But once the lover has been embraced by the presence of her Beloved, she turns away from everything that belongs to her. She knows that all that matters is her Beloved, and that her attention should remain only with Him. Everything that focuses on our self is an obstacle—al-Ansârî when discussing repentance warns against giving too much attention to our spiritual state.[11] And when Dhû-l-Nûn was asked about repentance he said, "The masses repent of their faults. The select repent of their neglect." While the novice turns away from faults and bad acts, the select have to turn away from anything that belongs to them, even "good and pious deeds." Sarraj finally quotes Dhû-l-Nûn as saying,

> What is sincerity for the seeker or novice is self-display for the knowers. When the knower has become firm and self-realized in that through which he draws near to God Most High and Transcendent—in the moment of his quest, in his beginning stage, upon his undertaking of offerings and pious deeds—when he has been encompassed by the lights of guidance, when providence has touched him, when he has been encircled by divine care, when his heart is witness to the majesty of his master, when he contemplates what God has fashioned and the eternity of his goodness, then he turns away from noticing, relying upon and attending to his pious deeds and acts and offerings, as he did a seeker and a beginner.[12]

It can be very difficult to realize that the very qualities and attitude that took us through a certain stage have to be left behind once that stage is passed. Inner work, attention to our faults and shadow qualities, is such an important part of our first years on the path. They are the tools, the rope and axe, that helped us up the mountain. To leave these qualities behind, to step into the vulnerability of the next stage, that of looking only to Him, can seem like deserting our own aspiration and commitment to the path. Surrendering the qualities that helped to heal and make us whole requires great trust and faith.

FANÂ

Any step beyond the self can evoke deep anxiety and fear. We hope for something tangible, some definite experience that can give us the reassurance we require if we are to leave behind the qualities that have taken us on our steep, demanding climb. But the path rarely provides what we expect. The path leads beyond the ego, beyond ourself. But where? And what do we experience of this shift? Often very little or nothing. As we walk along the path, daily life will continue to present us with the difficulties we have to learn from, challenges we have to confront. However, more and more our inner attention is absorbed somewhere else, but somewhere so different it leaves only a fine residue in our everyday consciousness. Outer life can become quite mundane, even boring, and our inner life may lack the psychological dramas that accompanied the time of intense inner work. The ego and mind, which always seek stimulation, do not know what to do with this shift. And because the notion of progress is so central to our culture, giving us a sense of purpose, even a "spiritual purpose," we can feel undermined if there is no apparent progress. For many years we worked hard upon ourself and were changed; now we just seem to remain with our old problems unresolved.

And more disturbing is the fact that our notion of ourself as a spiritual seeker becomes subverted. If *we* are not progressing, if *we* are not changing, in what way are we continuing on the path? Working on our own self was a tangible occupation; being absorbed in remembrance leaves few traces. The truth that the path is not about us, that we are not the wayfarer, is so contrary to all our expectations and spiritual conditioning that we cling to our old image of spiritual progress and thus can easily feel a failure.

The ego, whose sense of reality is based upon the illusion that it exists, cannot grasp the fact that the path is about *fanâ*, about becoming nothing. The ego's hold upon our consciousness is so strong that, even after years of meditation, we are often unable to digest this primal mystical truth. We may have heard about annihilation, but just as looking at a glass of wine does not prepare us for the experience of being drunk, thinking about *fanâ* can never prepare us for the experience of being nothing. The experience of *fanâ* is bewildering. Who or what is lost? Who or what remains behind? How can we be where we are not?

Slowly we are dissolved, slowly we matter less and less. Of what significance is it whether we have problems, insecurities, or phobias? Why should they be removed? We are just a human being like everyone else, except that in our heart of hearts a mystery is being revealed, a sweetness shared. Do we need to continue to struggle with ourself, seeking to resolve all our difficulties? Often it is simpler to learn to live with what we are and accept our ordinariness. In the midst of this humanness, the wonder of "I am He whom I love and He whom I love is me" unfolds unimpeded, and in this love the central part of ourself is being lost.

The idea that *fanâ* involves the death of the ego is a misunderstanding. There are moments of ecstasy in which the lover passes away in the presence of her Beloved. We emerge from these moments intoxicated and bewildered, knowing only that we were lost somewhere, that something was taken and something was given. But then we return to a self that still exists. This is the self which we inhabit in our daily life. Al-Junayd says that *fanâ* is not the passing away of our whole being in God's being, but the passing away of our will in the will of God. The ego remains, but it is surrendered to Him.

We need an ego in order to function in the world, and yet we hunger for the moments when we are lost, dissolved. We sense that somewhere an intoxication awaits us, and our daily duties can become merely tedious. But if we are to serve Him in His world we have to accept the ego with all of its limitations, even though we have glimpsed its illusory nature. We should not be attached to these moments of real awakening in which we are not. The following dream experience tells of the need to just continue our daily ego-bound life:

> As I was leaving at the end of a meditation meeting, a tall Russian man, plain and beautiful, came running to try and throw a bouquet of roses in my car. Some landed in the car and some fell on the road and were crushed. Then suddenly he stopped, and it was as if God came and got him. He was in bliss/ecstasy, with a huge smile on his face, and he was completely "gone." An orangish glow began, like a dome over his head, and he began to disappear, evaporate, beginning with the soles of his feet. It was as if he was getting sucked out through this dome of orange light. Then he was gone. It seemed this happened often, and that he reappeared, but one never knew when. I was there, waiting for him to reappear.
>
> Then I was telling my teacher about this, and he said, "Oh no, we don't do that." I thought at first he meant the disappearing, but then it seemed he was referring to our waiting for the man's return and my fascination with his disappearance.

This dream points to the wonder of *fanâ*, of dissolving in God. The Russian man who threw roses into the dreamer's car has been obliterated, has disappeared in the ecstasy of union. Al-Junayd describes three stages of *fanâ*. The first stage is the freedom from acting upon one's own desires in outer life. The second stage of *fanâ* is the freedom from pursuing the pleasures of the inner life, "even the sensation of pleasure in obedience to God's behests—so that you are exclusively His."[13] In these two stages what is annihilated is the ego's grip on the wayfarer; we are no longer the slave of its desires, and are thus able to give ourself more completely to our Beloved. But al-Junayd's third stage of *fanâ* is the obliteration of consciousness, when the worshiper herself is entirely overwhelmed by God. "At this stage you are obliterated and have eternal life in God.... Your physical being continues but your individuality has departed."[14] With a smile on his lips the Russian man has dissolved in God.

But this dream also illustrates one of the most confusing paradoxes of the path. The Russian man who is a part of the dreamer is lost in bliss, but the dreamer is left behind, and the dreamer is told neither to wait for his return nor to remain fascinated by his disappearance. She has to continue her daily life detached from the wonder that is taking place within her. Al-Junayd describes how one returns to the state of sobriety after the state of *fanâ*:

> He is himself, after he has not been truly himself. He is present in himself and in God after having been present in God and absent in himself. This is because he has left the intoxication of God's overwhelming *ghalaba* (victory), and comes to the clarity of sobriety....

Once more he assumes his individual attributes,
after *fanâ*.[15]

Reading al-Junayd one assumes that in this third
stage of *fanâ* the consciousness of the lover is completely
dissolved in her Beloved, from which state of divine
intoxication she returns to herself, to a state of sobriety.
Sometimes this is true and one experiences the complete
loss of self, and awakens only knowing that one has been
taken, intoxicated, into the presence of one's Beloved.
But the experience with the dreamer looking on as the
Russian man dissolves in bliss shows how *fanâ* can be
more complex; part of one is obliterated while at the same
time part remains behind. One is both absent and present
at the same time, both lost in God and bound within the
ego, both intoxicated and sober.

When one is totally dissolved one cannot function
in the outer world—there is no individual consciousness. This state of complete *fanâ* is therefore usually
limited to times of meditation or the nighttime. However, in the state of being absent and present at the
same time one can function in the outer world. In
fact one has to learn how to function with the clarity
of detachment from one's inner state, as this dream
suggests. The dreamer is told neither to be fascinated
with the man's disappearance nor to wait for his return.
One learns how to remain within the ego in a state
of sobriety, while an inner part of oneself is lost in
the light.

Only in a state of sobriety, remaining within the
limited consciousness of one's individual self, can one
be of service to the community, and Sufis are known
as "slaves of the One and servants of the many." We
are here to work in His world, to fulfill our daily duties
for His sake. It is for this reason that al-Junayd and

other Sufis stress the need for sobriety after the states of intoxication. Indeed it is said that the stage of servanthood comes after the stage of union. But al-Junayd also acknowledged that to be present and absent at the same time means a continual strain on the self. In a short poem he describes how these two opposites of separation and union co-exist:

> I have realized that which is within me.
> And my tongue has conversed with Thee in
> secret.
> And we are united in one respect,
> But we are separated in another.
> Although awe has hidden Thee from the
> glances of mine eye,
> Ecstasy has made Thee near to my innermost
> parts.[16]

The state of sobriety is sometimes described by the mystics as "the Second Separation," and this is the path the wayfarer walks, living within an ego which she knows to be limited and illusory. In "the First Separation" there was the longing for union and the need to be free of the ego. After tasting *fanâ* one has to embrace the ego anew, an ego which is changed and yet still the same. *Fanâ* is the annihilation of the will of the lover in the will of the Beloved, allowing us to fulfill our role as servant. To be His servant in His world we need to remain within the ego, and there is the added pain of *knowing* that somewhere we are free, somewhere we are together with our Beloved, and yet we have to consciously live in a state of limitation and separation. Al-Junayd says that one needs a special grace to endure this state of being both present and absent at the same time.

NOTHINGNESS AND THE EGO

During the first years on the path the ego-consciousness of the wayfarer becomes more balanced, more whole. Confronting our darkness, we find our own power, and can use this power to master our desires, to fight the greater *Jihâd* against our lower nature. Experiencing the freedom of self-mastery, we are able to live a fuller life, no longer caught in the darkness of our shadow or the chains of our ego desires. Our consciousness and freedom to participate in life expand, and we begin to feel the real meaning that is hidden in the unconscious. In meditation, dreams, and sometimes in waking life we feel the beauty and awe of our invisible Beloved; we touch the hem of His garment.

These years can be related to al-Junayd's first two stages of *fanâ*, and are a time of rewarding struggle against the ego and its dark twin. But gradually the wayfarer begins to sense that the real journey, the real meeting, is elsewhere. Then begin the experiences of being lost, being abandoned, of an abyss so deep there is nowhere to land. Sometimes the ego responds with horror as it glimpses the vastness of this emptiness, a landscape in which it knows it will find no fulfillment. The fear of the ego is real. Everything has just been a preparation for this next step, into the real *fanâ* of nothingness. The following dream experience is the dreamer's first *knowing* of this state:

> After meditating I lay down for a nap and dreamed that I am in a room full of people from the group. The teacher enters the room and it is as if he keeps entering the room, and then he enters me, he walks through, inside me. I feel fear. Then I remember that I am lying down in

> my bed taking a nap and I think that this really
> isn't happening, that I am dreaming. But at that
> point I know, with certainty, that I am not in
> bed but in that place where he has "entered"
> me. I am so shocked that I am not in my bed
> that I feel as if I am falling—it is like a "free fall"
> and instead of landing, I feel that I am fainting
> and I lose consciousness. After that there is just
> blackness and I don't remember anything.

This dream is actually not a dream but an experience of what is beyond the ego. The dreamer is in a place where the teacher enters her, the dimension of the soul where the true meeting of teacher and disciple takes place. Conscious that it is not a dream, she is taken beyond herself, into the blackness from which no news returns. This is the beginning of the real mystical journey, the journey into the uncreated void where His mysteries are revealed to Himself. Only there, in the nothingness beyond the ego, do we get a taste of our real nature, of our uncreated essence, "what we were before we were."

Returning from this other dimension *we know that we are not*, and this has a profound effect upon the ego. The inner structure and autonomy of the ego can be disturbed to such a degree that if the wayfarer had not been prepared by years of meditation and spiritual practice, and were not held by the energy of the path, she could become seriously unbalanced. Even then we have to adjust to this fundamental shift which affects our entire sense of ourself. We have to live within the ego in everyday life, but more and more we become aware of its illusory nature. We become aware that we are not, just as we sense that we are living in a world of illusion. This shift in self-awareness usually happens at the borders of consciousness—the ego structure is subverted from within, and we do not have to directly confront the absolute nature of this change. We only sense that the ego is no longer the dominant force in our life—that its fulfillment is no longer a primary drive.

Gradually we glimpse that the ego is just an actor on a small stage, and we feel the enormous space that surrounds this stage. Our years of individuation enabled the ego to act its role to the full, play its part in life. But now we realize the limited nature of this stage, feel the confines of our ego world. Its colors appear muted at best, except in those moments when the beyond is reflected, when we see His face here in this world. Only sometimes are we given a taste of what is real.

Each in our own way we are taken beyond the ego and learn to adjust to a life in which our "I" is no longer the central figure. There is a subtle shift away from the clear-cut delineations of conscious life into a strangely undefinable state. Without the opposites of subject and object, of "I" and "not I," this new awareness can be as disturbing as it is wonderful. Something is given; an opening has been made into the mystery of His presence. While writing this passage I received a letter from a friend which movingly describes this transition taking place within him:

> Even more than ever I know so little about who I am, what I am doing, where I am going, etc. There are frequently those times when I am called upon to give a response or make a decision, but there is not the old "me" present to look to for a response. At these moments I experience a momentary fright, because I have

no answer. It is like I have exhaled and am unsure whether a subsequent inhale will be offered by That Other. Almost all the time, after but a pause, there is an answer! On those occasions when there is no forthcoming answer I have gotten accustomed to saying, "I don't know." On occasion I become afraid of this, but most of the time I just do what I am urged to do (or it is just done) while I try to remember the Beloved as much as I can. Is this what is called being one of His idiots?

More and more I am neither good nor bad, but feel I just am. This has proved to be difficult for me as I have striven all my life to be good. It is as if I have loved white all my life and been repelled by black, but now must accept gray, which does not have the obvious brilliance of white. But, as I have discovered, gray has a hidden depth which makes it far more valuable than white. I see how all the opposites constellate to form a center, a resolution. In this center there is a hidden door which leads out of the paradox. It is in this center where His spark, His infinitude are found. As in looking into an enormous spiral, only when one looks into the very center is infinity revealed.

Several months ago, I had a wonderful, gentle experience of clarity in my heart. I called it "the clarity" and it lived in my heart. I looked to it, and nurtured it while it chose to stay. It was beautiful. Like all my states, it didn't last. I let go of it and another state followed, but not nearly so delicate or nice. I wrote then, "There is a Clarity within. It is not me, but it is not different from me. It is essentially me, but without any color, flavor, or style, such as a personality has. It is like pure water, as compared to any other beverage which has color or flavor; it is clear."

All our life we have been the actor. We still have a part to play, duties to fulfill. But slowly something else comes to life, which "is not me, but it is not different from me." This essential self does not belong to the limitations of this world, nor to its definitions; unlike a personality it is "without any color, flavor, or style." One of the qualities of *fanâ* is a return to this essential purity of a self without delineation. This is the invisible center of our being that belongs to a different dimension, a oneness without the distinctions of separation.

In the dimension beyond the stage, in the dynamic darkness that surrounds it, there is no actor, no sense of self caught in the spotlights of consciousness. Without an actor there are no words to hear, no story to tell, just an overwhelming feeling of something primary and powerful. Here is the uncreated emptiness, infinite and eternal. And the wayfarer has to live with a dawning consciousness of this other realm, a consciousness in which she is not: "There is no dervish, or if there is a dervish that dervish is not there."[17]

Finally the ego has to confront and accept the inevitable. I once spent a whole summer adjusting to the fact that I knew "I" did not exist. This may sound a strange paradox, but I felt my ego reconciling itself with the black hole that was now at its center. I still have my part to play in life, my role on the small stage of daily existence, but my ego has to contain the knowledge of its own non-existence. This was a very puzzling and bewildering period, as I felt my ego struggle and slowly come to terms with its own illusory nature. The ego did adjust, the stage passed, and life continues. The wonder of the path is that it prepares us for these transitions and gradually guides us through them. Mystical life may appear to be full of contradictions, but that is only to the mind. The path takes us closer to the essential simplicity of what is, and offers us the tremendous freedom of knowing our own non-existence. And our daily life continues. My friend ended his letter:

> More and more there are no answers. I am just thankful for those moments when He visits and both hurts and sends into bliss those most tender places deep in my heart. The tears that flow in those moments feel infinitely sweet.

NOTES

INTRODUCTION

1. Mechthild of Magdeburg, quoted by Carol Lee Flinders, *Enduring Grace*, p. 53.

THE PRAYER OF THE HEART

1. Quoted by Al-Qushayri, *Principles of Sufism*, trans. B. R. von Schlegell, pp. 275–276.
2. Annemarie Schimmel, *Mystical Dimensions of Islam*, p. 148.
3. Quoted by Schimmel, *Mystical Dimensions of Islam*, p. 150.
4. Rûmî, *Mathnawi*, quoted by R. A. Nicholson, *The Mystics of Islam*, p. 113.
5. Quoted by Claude Addas, *Quest for the Red Sulphur: The Life of Ibn 'Arabî*, p. 61.
6. Al-Qushayri, *Principles of Sufism*, p. 278.
7. Jîlî, quoted by R. S. Bhatnagar, *Dimensions of Classical Sufi Thought*, p. 120.
8. Trans. Coleman Barks, *Delicious Laughter*, p. 14. Rûmî's image of the baker reflects a tradition which relates, "When a servant whom God loves prays to Him, He says, 'O Gabriel, delay answering the need of my servant, for I love hearing his voice.' When a servant whom God dislikes prays to Him, God says, 'O Gabriel, answer My servant's need, for I dislike hearing his voice.'" Quoted

by Al-Qushayri, *Principles of Sufism*, p. 278.

9. Quoted by Al-Qushayri, *Principles of Sufism*, p. 278.

10. *The Cloud of Unknowing*, quoted by T. S. Eliot, "Little Gidding," l. 238.

11. Quoted by Al-Qushayri, *Principles of Sufism*, p. 282.

12. Quoted by Schimmel, *Mystical Dimensions of Islam*, p. 165.

13. "The Dry Salvages," l. 93.

14. Fakhruddîn 'Irâqî, *Divine Flashes*, trans. Peter Lamborn Wilson, p. 116.

15. Al-Ghazzâlî, quoted by Schimmel, *Mystical Dimensions of Islam*, p. 139.

16. *Divine Flashes*, pp. 118–119.

LISTENING

1. *Rilke's Book of Hours*, trans. Anita Barrows and Joanna Macy, I, 45.

2. *Light Upon Light*, trans. Andrew Harvey, p. 99.

3. Irina Tweedie, *Daughter of Fire*, p. 466.

4. *Nag Hammadi Codices*, VI.55.19–22, trans. Peter Kingsley, "Knowing Beyond Knowing," p. 23.

5. *Corpus Hermeticum* 10.17 and *Asclepius* 3, trans. Peter Kingsley, "Knowing Beyond Knowing," p. 24.

6. Bhai Sahib, quoted by Tweedie, p. 148.

7. Tweedie, p. 145.

POWER & SPIRITUAL LIFE I

1. *"Whoso Knoweth Himself…,"* Beshara Publications, p. 27.

2. "Impotent people cannot have *Brahma Vidya* [knowledge of Brahma], men or women." Bhai Sahib, quoted

in Tweedie, p. 497. Also "A man who is impotent can never be a Saint or a Yogi. Women too can be impotent. The Creative Energy of God which manifests itself in its lowest aspect as procreative instinct is the most powerful thing in human beings, men and women alike." Tweedie, p. 149.

3. Trans. Coleman Barks, *One-Handed Basket Weaving*, p. 112.

4. Rûmî, trans. William Chittick, *The Sufi Path of Love*, p. 339.

5. See Vaughan-Lee, *The Lover and the Serpent*, p. 67.

6. *The Secrets of God's Mystical Oneness*, Ebn-e Monavvar, trans. John O'Kane, p. 486.

7. Bk. II, 1, trans. Shree Purohit Swami and W. B. Yeats.

8. *The Secrets of God's Mystical Oneness*, p. 455.

9. Rûmî, trans. Andrew Harvey, *Light Upon Light*, p. 79.

10. *St. Matthew*, 7:7–8.

POWER & SPIRITUAL LIFE II

1. Quoted by Bhatnagar, p. 82.

2. *Zen Flesh, Zen Bones*, compiled by Paul Reps, pp.143–144.

3. Reps, *Zen Flesh, Zen Bones*, p. 147.

4. Much of Carl Jung's work explores this process (which he termed individuation), particularly as it is imaged in alchemical symbolism. For example, see *Collected Works* vol. 5, *Symbols of Transformation*, or *Collected Works* vol. 14, *Mysterium Coniunctionis.*

5. Unpublished quotation.

6. Reps, *Zen Flesh, Zen Bones*, p. 141.

7. Reps, *Zen Flesh, Zen Bones*, p. 142.

8. Tweedie, p. 104.

9. See "Two Wings To Fly" in Vaughan-Lee, *Paradoxes of Love*, pp. 96-116, for a description of masculine and feminine approaches to spiritual life.

10. See Vaughan-Lee, *The Bond with the Beloved*, p. 123.

11. Tweedie, p. 365.

12. Quoted by Richard Power, *Falling Awake*, p. 79.

13. Quoted in *Travelling the Path of Love*, ed. Vaughan-Lee, p. 84.

14. Tweedie, p. 821.

15. Nasr, quoted by Schimmel, *Mystical Dimensions of Islam*, p. 271.

16. Schimmel, *Mystical Dimensions of Islam*, p. 271.

17. Chittick, *The Sufi Path of Knowledge*, p. 318.

18. Ibn 'Arabî, quoted by Chittick, *The Sufi Path of Knowledge*, p. 317.

19. Tweedie, p. 165.

20. Quoted by William Chittick, *The Sufi Path of Love*, p. 162.

21. *The Concept of Sainthood in Early Islamic Mysticism, Two Works by al-Hakîm at-Tirmidhî*, trans. Bernd Radtke and John O'Kane, p. 90.

THE ABYSS OF ABANDONMENT

1. Trans. Coleman Barks, *Birdsong*, p. 13.

2. Trans. Coleman Barks, *One-Handed Basket Weaving*, p. 112.

3. Rûmî, trans. Coleman Barks, *We Are Three*, p. 30.

4. Trans. Coleman Barks, *The Essential Rumi*, p. 243.

5. *The Concept of Sainthood in Early Islamic Mysticism*, Bernd Radtke and John O'Kane, p. 205.

6. Quoted by Al-Qushayri, *Principles of Sufism*, trans. B. R. von Schlegell, p. 185.

7. *St. Matthew*, 27:46.

8. *Tao Te Ching*, trans. Stephen Mitchell, 22.

9. Rûmî, trans. Coleman Barks, *The Essential Rumi*, p. 270.

10. *The Conference of the Birds*, trans. Afkham Darbandi and Dick Davis, p. 61.

11. *The Conference of the Birds*, p. 66.

12. *The Conference of the Birds*, pp. 66–67.

13. Tweedie, p. 373.

14. Tweedie, p. 551.

15. Trans. Andrew Harvey, *Light Upon Light*, p. 98.

16. Quoted by Louis Massignon, *The Passion of al-Hallâj*, vol. 1, p. 609.

17. Trans. Coleman Barks, *We Are Three*, p. 30.

FORGETFULNESS

1. Quoted by Chittick, *The Sufi Path of Knowledge*, p. 296.

2. Trans. Andrew Harvey, *Light Upon Light*, pp. 18–19.

3. Quoted by Chittick, *The Sufi Path of Knowledge*, p. 195.

4. *anyone lived in a pretty how town.*

5. Quoted by Chittick, *The Sufi Path of Knowledge*, p. 296.

6. Deception is also a divine quality: "They deceived and God deceived, and God is the best of deceivers" (Qur'an 3:54).

7. *The Precious Pearl*, trans. Nicholas Heer, p. 37.

8. 'Attâr, *The Book of Secrets*, trans. from the French Lynn Finegan, ch. I, ll. 32–35.

9. 'Attâr, *The Book of Secrets*, ch. I, l. 22.

10. Ibn 'Arabî, quoted by Chittick, *The Sufi Path of Knowledge*, p. 238.

11. Ibn 'Arabî, quoted by Chittick, *The Sufi Path of Knowledge*, p. 239.

12. *Hadîth qudsî.*

13. *Nawâdir al-usûl* (=The Rarest of Traditions), Tradition

no. 287 on *The Word of Godfearing (taqwâ) and the Form of its Meaning within the Heart*, unpublished trans. Sara Sviri.

14. Quoted by Massignon, vol. 3, p. 353.

THE INVISIBLE CENTER

1. Trans. A. G. Ravan Farhadî, *Abdullâh Ansârî of Herât, An Early Sufi Master*, p. 110.

2. Tweedie, p. x.

3. See "The Transformation of the Shadow" in Vaughan-Lee, *Catching the Thread*, pp. 50–76.

4. Trans. A. G. Ravan Farhadî, *Abdullâh Ansârî of Herât, An Early Sufi Master*, pp. 108–109.

5. The transformation of the shadow can only be partial, as the ego needs the shadow as an unconscious balance.

6. For an exploration of the relationship with the inner partner, see Vaughan-Lee, *Catching the Thread*, pp. 105–145.

7. Written in the tenth century, *The Book of Flashes* (*Kitâb al-Luma'*) contains one of the first systematic expositions of Sufism as a way of life and thought.

8. Quoted by Sarraj, *The Book of Flashes, Early Islamic Mysticism*, trans. Michael Sells, p. 199.

9. Quoted by Sarraj, *The Book of Flashes, Early Islamic Mysticism*, p. 199.

10. Quoted by Sarraj, *The Book of Flashes, Early Islamic Mysticism*, p. 200.

11. *The Hundred Grounds*, trans. Ravan Farhadî, p. 64.

12. Quoted by Sarraj, *The Book of Flashes, Early Islamic Mysticism*, p. 200.

13. Quoted by Ali Hassan Abdel-Kader, *The Life, Personality and Writings of Al-Junayd*, p. 81.

14. Quoted by Abdel-Kader, p. 81.

15. Quoted by Abdel-Kader, p. 90.
16. Quoted by Abdel-Kader, p. 91.
17. Rûmî, trans. Coleman Barks, *We Are Three*, p. 30.

BIBLIOGRAPHY

Abdel-Kader, Ali Hassan. *The Life, Personality and Writings of Al-Junayd.* London: Luzac & Company, 1976.

Addas, Claude. *Quest for the Red Sulphur: The Life of Ibn 'Arabî.* Cambridge: The Islamic Texts Society, 1994.

Al-Qushayri. *Principles of Sufism.* Trans. B. R. von Schlegell. Berkeley: Mizan Press, 1990.

Attâr, Farîd ud-Dîn. *The Conference of the Birds.* Trans. Afkham Darbandi and Dick Davis. London: Penguin Books, 1984.

—. *The Book of Secrets.* Trans. Lynn Finegan. Unpublished.

Bhatnagar, R. S. *Dimensions of Classical Sufi Thought.* Delhi: Motilal Banarsidass, 1984.

Chittick, William C. *The Sufi Path of Love.* Albany: State University of New York Press, 1983.

—. *The Sufi Path of Knowledge.* Albany: State University of New York Press, 1989.

Ebn-e Monavvar, M. *The Secrets of God's Mysical Oneness (Asrar al Tawhid).* Trans. John O'Kane. Costa Mesa, California: Mazda Publishers, 1992.

Fakhruddîn 'Irâqî. *Divine Flashes.* Trans. Peter Lamborn Wilson. New York: Paulist Press, 1982.

Hâfiz, Muhammad Shamsuddîn. *The Green Sea of Heaven.* Trans. Elizabeth Gray. Ashland: White Cloud Press, 1995.

Harvey, Andrew. *Light Upon Light: Inspirations from RUMI.* Berkeley: North Atlantic Books, 1996.

Heer, Nicholas. *The Precious Pearl.* Albany: State University of New York Press, 1979.

Ibn 'Arabî. *"Whoso Knoweth Himself..."* Oxford: Beshara Publications, 1976.

Jung, C. G. *Collected Works.* London: Routledge & Kegan Paul.

Kingsley, Peter. "Knowing Beyond Knowing." In *Parabola,* vol. xx no. 1, Spring 1997, pp. 21–24.

Massignon, Louis. *The Passion of al-Hallâj.* Princeton: Princeton University Press, 1982.

Mitchell, Stephen, trans. *Tao Te Ching.* New York: Harper & Row, 1988.

Nicholson, R. A. *Studies in Islamic Mysticism.* Cambridge: Cambridge University Press, 1921.

O'Kane, John, and Bernd Radtke. *The Concept of Sainthood in Early Islamic Mysticism.* Richmond, Surrey: Curzon Press, 1996.

Power, Richard, ed. *Great Song: The Life and Teachings of Joe Miller.* Athens, GA: Maypop Books, 1993.

Ravan Farhadî, A. G. *Abdullâh Ansârî of Herât.* Richmond, Surrey: Curzon Press, 1996.

Reps, Paul. *Zen Flesh, Zen Bones.* Harmondsworth: Penguin Books, 1971.

Rilke, Rainer Maria. *Rilke's Book of Hours.* Trans. Anita Burrows and Joanna Macy. New York: Putnam's, 1996.

Rûmî, Jelaluddin. *We Are Three.* Trans. Coleman Barks. Athens, GA: Maypop Books, 1987.

—. *Delicious Laughter.* Trans. Coleman Barks. Athens, GA: Maypop Books, 1990.

—. *Like This.* Trans. Coleman Barks. Athens, GA: Maypop Books, 1990.

—. *One-Handed Basket Weaving.* Trans. Coleman Barks. Athens, GA: Maypop Books, 1991.

—. *Birdsong.* Trans. Coleman Barks. Athens, GA: Maypop Books, 1993.

—. *The Essential Rumi.* Trans. Coleman Barks with John Moyne. New York: HarperCollins, 1995.

Schimmel, Annemarie. *Mystical Dimensions of Islam.* Chapel Hill: University of North Carolina Press, 1975.

Sells, Michael, ed. *Early Islamic Sufism.* New Jersey: Paulist Press, 1996.

Tweedie, Irina. *Daughter of Fire: A Diary of a Spiritual Training with a Sufi Master.* Nevada City: Blue Dolphin Publishing, 1986.

Vaughan-Lee, Llewellyn. *The Lover and the Serpent: Dreamwork within a Sufi Tradition.* Shaftesbury: Element Books, 1989.

—. *The Bond with the Beloved.* Inverness, California: Golden Sufi Center, 1993.

—. *In the Company of Friends: Dreamwork in a Sufi Group.* Inverness, California: Golden Sufi Center, 1994.

—. *Sufism, The Transformation of the Heart.* Inverness, California: Golden Sufi Center, 1995.

—. *Catching the Thread: Sufism, Dreamwork and Jungian Psychology.* Inverness, California: Golden Sufi Center, 1998.

—, ed. *Travelling the Path of Love, Sayings of Sufi Masters.* Inverness, California: Golden Sufi Center, 1995.

Yeats, W. B., trans. (with Shree Purohit Swami). *The Ten Principal Upanishads.* London: Faber and Faber, 1937.

INDEX

ACKNOWLEDGMENTS

For permission to use copyrighted material, the author gratefully wishes to acknowledge: HarperCollins Publishers, Inc., for permission to quote from *Tao Te Ching* by Lao Tzu, a new English version, with foreword and notes by Stephen Mitchell, translation (© 1988) by Stephen Mitchell; White Cloud Press, P.O. Box 3400, Ashland OR 97520, www.whitecloudpress.com, for permission to quote from *The Green Sea of Heaven* translated by Elizabeth T. Gray, Jr. (© 1995); Paulist Press Inc., for permission to quote from *Early Islamic Mysticism* translated, edited, and with an introduction by Michael A. Sells, (© 1996) by Michael A. Sells; Putnam Berkley, a division of Penguin Putnam Inc., for permission to quote from "Du kommst und gehst.../ You come and go," from *Rilke's Book of Hours: Love Poems to God* by Rainer Maria Rilke translated by Anita Barrows and Joanna Macy, translation (© 1996) by Anita Barrows and Joanna Macy; Curzon, for permission to quote from *Abdullâh Ansârî of Herât* by Ravan Farhadî, and *The Concept of Sainthood in Early Islamic Mysticism* by John O'Kane and Bernd Radtke; State University of New York Press, for permission to quote from *The Precious Pearl* translated by Nicholas Heer; North Atlantic Books, for permission to quote from *Light Upon Light: Inspirations from RUMI* by Andrew Harvey; Center of Iranian Studies, Columbia University, for permission to quote from *The Secrets of God's Mystical Oneness (Asrar al Tawhid)* by Ebn-e Monavvar translated by

John O'Kane, Biblioteca Persica (© 1997); Penguin Books Ltd., for permission to quote sixteen lines (pp 61, 66, 67) from *The Conference of the Birds* by Farîd ud-Dîn Attâr, translated by Afkham Darbandi and Dick Davis (Penguin Classics, 1984), (© 1984) by Afkham Darbandi and Dick Davis; Mizan Press for permission to quote from *Principles of Sufism* by al-Qushayri, trans. B.R. von Schlegell, Mizan Press (© 1990).

LLEWELLYN VAUGHAN-LEE, Ph.D., has followed the Naqshbandi Sufi Path since he was nineteen. In 1991 he moved from London to northern California, where he now lives with his wife and two children. He lectures throughout the United States and Europe.

THE GOLDEN SUFI CENTER is a California Religious Non-Profit Corporation dedicated to making the teachings of the Naqshbandi Sufi Path available to all seekers. For further information about the activities of the Center and Llewellyn Vaughan-Lee's lectures, write to:

The Golden Sufi Center
P.O. Box 428
Inverness, California 94937-0428

tel: (415) 663-8773
fax: (415) 663-9128
email: goldensufi@aol.com
website: http//www.goldensufi.org

OTHER TITLES PUBLISHED BY
THE GOLDEN SUFI CENTER

BY LLEWELLYN VAUGHAN-LEE

THE BOND WITH THE BELOVED
The Mystical Relationship of the Lover and the Beloved

•

IN THE COMPANY OF FRIENDS
Dreamwork within a Sufi Group

•

TRAVELLING THE PATH OF LOVE
Sayings of Sufi Masters

•

SUFISM, THE TRANSFORMATION OF THE HEART

•

THE PARADOXES OF LOVE

•

THE FACE BEFORE I WAS BORN
A Spiritual Autobiography

•

CATCHING THE THREAD
Sufism, Dreamwork & Jungian Psychology

BY IRINA TWEEDIE

DAUGHTER OF FIRE
A Diary of a Spiritual Training with a Sufi Master

BY SARA SVIRI

THE TASTE OF HIDDEN THINGS
Images of the Sufi Path

BY PETER KINGSLEY

IN THE DARK PLACES OF WISDOM